Contents

Acknowledgements

The Programme Development Unit of the Schools Council Research and Development Project in Compensatory Education wish to acknowledge the help given them in the early development and evaluation of draft material by Miss Ena Grey, former Organiser for Infant Education, Glamorgan Education Authority, and Miss Evelyn Thompson, former Headteacher, Cimla Infant School, Glamorgan, and the former education authorities of Birmingham, Bristol, Burton on Trent, Glamorgan and Swansea.

Preface

In November 1967 the Department of Education of the University College of Swansea, with the financial support of the Schools Council, began a research and development project in compensatory education. The aims of the project were threefold:
(a) to provide screening techniques to enable children in need of special help to be identified at an early age;
(b) to make longitudinal studies of infant children in deprived areas, with particular reference to their emotional development and response to schooling;
(c) to develop teaching programmes for helping culturally deprived children at the infant school stage.
Since 1969 the Programme Development Unit of the Schools Council Research and Development Project in Compensatory Education has concentrated its efforts on preparing materials, of which this handbook represents a major part, in order to foster language development among deprived children. Three reasons lay behind this decision.

First, a review of the literature showed that most studies pointed to language 'deficit' or 'difference' as the key to the poor development of many deprived children.

Much of this literature was North American in origin, and consequently was set in a different culture from our own. But the early work of the Project's other Units, concerned with children in this country, was also pointing clearly in the same direction. This was the second reason for emphasising language skills.

The third reason was based not on research, but on opinion. The Unit had established a number of teacher groups from schools in deprived areas. Early discussions in these groups soon underlined the overriding concern of these teachers about the inadequate language skills of their children. The teachers wished to develop materials and methods which would help remove this language inadequacy.

The Unit decided, therefore, to aim at facilitating the development of a set of key language skills which had been identified by the teacher groups as particularly important. Although these skills do not run counter to research findings, not everyone will agree that the seven skills identified are the most effective way of analysing the language process. But they are the skills which emerged from the group discussions as those which teachers of deprived children see as central to the needs of their children.

Having decided the target of the language programme, the groups turned their attention to the question of method. Discussions soon revealed that the approach found in American language programmes for deprived children—such as the Peabody Language Development Kit—was too detailed and prescriptive, and was alien to the atmosphere of the British infant school. British teachers did *not* want a formalised programme. They *did* want a general guide or set of ideas which could be adapted, developed and extended to suit their own particular methods.

Two years of intensive work led to the production of a set of materials and the associated handbook which were then tried out in infant schools in four education authorities. There were two purposes to these trials. One was to gain the opinion of teachers other than those involved in preparing the materials. To do this, a short questionnaire was constructed which asked teachers to evaluate the materials using a number of dimensions.

The results of this field testing are set out in Appendix 2, page 86. The second purpose was to invite constructive criticism which would enable the material to be improved further. The testers responded well to our invitation, and their current suggestions for materials reflect some detailed changes from the experimental set.

The handbook is both a guide to ways of developing in the infant school the language skills identified by our teacher groups and a collection of suggestions for language games. These reflect the theme of the project in that they are not intended as an ideal set of activities, but as examples of teacher-developed activities and materials which infants' teachers can use as a basis for further development to meet their own needs.

Phillip Williams

Introduction   The need for oral language

In the section on oral language the Bullock Report states: 'we cannot emphasise too strongly our conviction of its importance in the education of the child'. This conviction is supported by studies made amongst children experiencing educational problems and by the opinions and feelings voiced in many teacher discussion groups. Indeed, slow or inadequate language development not only handicaps a child's education but causes difficulty in his whole emotional, intellectual and social development.

The acquisition of the mother tongue in the first few years of life is remarkable considering the complexity of language. The ability to internalise and reproduce a human language is a precious gift; normally children learn their language quickly in the first few years of their life, but the longer this learning is delayed the more difficult the intricate patterns of language are to master. The most fortunate of our children will arrive at schoool at the age of five with very wide patterns of language and understanding already mastered, and education in school will be built on to this firm foundation. The surest way of learning the mother tongue is to be exposed to a wide sample of language during the early years; to hear many people speaking around you, to be able at a very early age to enter into this conversation, to make mistakes and have them corrected in a secure background, to hear different forms of speech, casual and more formal, precise and discursive, and, most important of all, to have your own successful efforts at expressing yourself rewarded in a variety of ways. The fortunate child hears adults in the home speaking to members of the family, to friends, to officials, to people in shops; he or she hears discussions, descriptions, commands, persuasions and disagreements; his or her own efforts at speech are encouraged and supported, and throughout the very early years the facility for language develops in complexity.

The disadvantaged child will arrive at school with less of this experience and so with less ability for self-expression; little is to be gained by either the teacher or the child in pursuing literacy, numeracy and other areas of education if there cannot be accelerated development of oral language as soon as possible.

How to encourage spoken language?

How can spoken language be encouraged? The best way, plainly, would be by replacing experience which should have come from the home with similar experience at school. Unfortunately, conditions in the infant school do not allow for consistent concentration of attention on one child. Language in the home is learnt by a child from several surrounding adults, and it is very difficult to replace this in school where a few adults are in communication with a large number of children. Talk within the peer group is sociable and necessary but it does not develop the spoken language as adult conversation would do. It is of the greatest importance to have as much conversation as possible but in school conditions this alone cannot be enough. It is important to develop listening skills in the child but listening alone is not enough. The problem becomes increasingly difficult as the child becomes older. Even in 'discussion' lessons in the upper juniors or in the secondary school an individual child will have very little time to speak and those who do so are likely to be the ones who find self-expression relatively easy. Even in a group categorised as slow learners there will be those with a greater language facility than others and these will be the ones who 'discuss'. Time is always limited; it takes a lot of persuasion to draw out those who have difficulty in expressing themselves and perhaps then only for a few moments. The problem of *teaching* the oral mother tongue has not been solved.

Identifying seven language skills
This book does not claim to have produced an answer but it does contain a set of positive guidelines on which the teacher can base his or her approach. First of all, seven important aspects of spoken language are identified. These aspects, or skills as they are referred to, are not necessarily placed in order of priority or chronological sequence although the first one named—listening—is fundamental to language. Many children who hear quite acutely have, for one reason or another, already 'switched off' at the age of five; perhaps they have already learned to retire into themselves rather than hear what they do not want to hear—quarrels, violent language, abuse, blame from adults, themselves under great stress. Perhaps they have ceased to listen to television programmes that are on the whole time and which they do not understand, or conversation which excludes them and in which they are not expected to join. Perhaps there is no satisfaction for them in paying attention to the world of sound. The noise level in city life is high; some children just do not want to hear it any longer, but would rather live an inner life of make-believe.

Naming may seem to many to be a very basic ability but the infant teacher will often find that she is dealing with language development at a very basic level. A child who has not been in the habit of talking simply uses gestures to indicate needs. Naming is one of the early language skills. The baby learns to say Mum, Nan, ball or cup and these terms often include a wealth of meaning: 'Cuddle me Mum (or Nan)', 'I want my ball (or cup)'—the ability to name is a big step forward. The disadvantaged child may not have discovered the art of naming or may simply not know what a lot of things are—adults often presume that the child has some concept of 'boat', 'sea', 'train'; for the very restricted child this may not be so.

Describing and categorising may seem at first to be very similar skills and they do overlap in concept, but a distinction can be made. The ability to describe lies at the heart of a great deal of imagination and creative thought whilst the ability to categorise lies at the heart of many processes of reason and of scientific development. Sequencing and reasoning will also be seen as logical and orderly processes, whilst denoting position may again seem to be

8

very simple and basic. The seven aspects are not intended to be seen in isolation; each is dependent on the others and they will often overlap. This is the nature of language; it is not a simple aggregation of separate processes.

Teachers may with reason see other ways of analysing language processes and may wish to make other distinctions; those who contributed to the work described in this book defined skills which seemed clear and important to them. The interdependence of the processes is acknowledged by them in the fact that several of the games described in the book are included under more than one heading—a game which helps to form ideas of categorisation may also help to develop reasoning skills, for example.

The aim of the book is to give specific guidelines to language activity. Oral language is learned by talk but there is an instinctive and rational doubt in teachers' minds of the value of general 'chat' in a school situation; conversation with a well-informed adult on a one-to-one basis is indeed helpful but a more realistic substitute must be found. This book outlines specific groups of games which will give children a focus of talk and an opportunity to develop important skills. At the same time the teacher is helped to consider the important skills involved in spoken language and to have clear objectives in a plan of work.

One of the difficulties with which the teacher must contend is the vague nature of terms such as 'language deprivation' and 'language skills'. Individually, we think we know what we mean and we can all recognise a case of extreme language deprivation when we meet one, but exact criteria and measurement are elusive. Many educationalists, including teachers, psychologists and linguists, have attempted to define and analyse language and to specify teaching objectives. Virtually all attempts have had to be modified and adapted in the light of research. This is hardly surprising when one considers the complex nature of language. The difficulty of exact definition must not, however, become the excuse for us to do nothing and just hope for the best; here this book offers some principles and some guidelines for the teacher to work on. Its last section includes a checklist of language skills which can be used both to identify weaknesses in a child's linguistic ability and as some measure of progress. Whether this last section is used diagnostically or as a record, it should help the teacher to consider the problem in a more clearly defined way so that the component parts which contribute to oral facility can be assessed separately.

Language development in context

The fostering of language should be seen in the context of other well-known educational considerations. For, while special attention to language develop-ment is likely to be of considerable effect as an approach to the educational problems raised by deprivation, this cannot be seen as a complete solution in itself. Despite the close relationship between the child's language competence and general progress in school, other important social and educational needs must also be considered. These are:

Social and emotional needs: the child needs to establish a friendly and secure relationship with other children. He or she also needs to develop a relationship with the teacher to help adjust to new and complex situations and to make full use of the learning opportunities in the school.

Creative and imaginative needs: it is important for the child to have the opportunity to explore freely through games, art, craft, P.E., music and drama the worlds of reality and fantasy. Through these activities he or she can learn to understand the environment, find emotional satisfaction and personal fulfilment.

Mathematical experiences: although stress is laid on language, including the language of mathematics, the child needs plenty of practical experience of sorting, arranging, measuring, weighing and assessing to extend a knowledge of his or her environment and to lay the foundation of future mathematical discoveries and concepts.

The teacher's role

The teacher's own part in this language development cannot be overemphasised. She may be the only adult present with the children for much of the day; she is right in feeling that opportunities for discovery or long periods of time spent in giving directions to the children are not enough; she has a vital, unique but strangely difficult to define role. Those who are not widely experienced will need some advice and guidance as to how they should become parent, friend, adviser and instructor to a group of demanding children, without forgetting those who do not demand but who may need even more attention. Practical guidance on how to encourage aspects of language is not easily found and it is not easy to design materials or situations which will increase oral facility. It is not suggested that any one teacher with a class or group will want to work through these games, hoping that each aspect of language will be satisfactorily 'learnt' as he or she goes along. It is hoped that the teacher will have time to consider each section thoughtfully and decide which of the activities will best meet the needs of the children and which are most suited to the possibilities of the situation. Most British schools give very considerable latitude to the individual teacher to use and develop ideas and materials in a way most suited to a class. For this reason the materials should be used flexibly in language development.

Conclusion

As individuals we need to become more aware of language if we are to try to help children in this essential way. To quote from the Bullock report again: 'As children grow older the school makes progressively greater demands on their language. The teacher should have an explicit knowledge of the nature of these demands to enable her to help the child who is finding it difficult to meet them.'

This book is intended to help the teacher understand more of the processes of language so that she or he may guide the child towards the development and enrichment of spoken language.

Pamela Schaub

Deputy Head of Peckham School; former team member of the Schools' Council Linguistics and English Teaching: Initial Literacy Project, and one of the authors of the Breakthrough to Literacy Scheme.

PART 1

Seven language skills:
development through activities and materials

Introduction

Language skills

Part 1 of the handbook discusses some of the likely weaknesses in the language of the disadvantaged child and suggests activities which can help to overcome them.

Language is broken down into the following identifiable skills, each of which is considered in detail in a separate chapter: 1 Listening, 2 Naming, 3 Categorising, 4 Describing, 5 Denoting position, 6 Sequencing, and 7 Reasoning.

It must be stressed that this breakdown is one of convenience; language is more than the accumulation of separate skills. It is helpful, however, to study each separately so that specific aims and relevant activities can be highlighted. This assists the teacher in recognizing particular weaknesses in the disadvantaged child's language and in promoting related activities to remedy them.

To say this does not imply that each skill should always be covered in isolation. There is considerable overlap of skills as, for example, in the statement: 'If you take away the red block, it (the tower) will fall.' Here one can identify the interplay of several skills: naming ('block'), describing ('red'), sequencing ('take away' followed by 'will fall'), and reasoning ('If . . .'). Similarly, there is almost always overlap between naming and categorising. 'Let's put the cat and the dog and the horse together because they're all animals' involves both naming the members of the category and labelling the category itself. Because of the unified nature of spoken language, overlap cannot be avoided and, indeed, should be encouraged so that new or unused skills become incorporated into the child's normal language.

Aims and approaches

The language skills which are likely to present the greatest difficulty and require special attention are those termed categorising, denoting position, sequencing and reasoning (see chapters 3, 5, 6 and 7).

These skills involve the use of relational words such as under, between (relations of position), before, after (relations of time) and if, but (relations of cause, effect and conditions). There are reasonably few relational words in our language, but they are crucial to language development and are difficult for the young child to understand and use appropriately. Relational words can help the child to perceive his or her own complex surroundings not as a number of isolated and disconnected parts (which can be named, using content words), but as an organised pattern of interrelated objects and events.

In contrast to the small number of relational words, there are many content words, such as dog, chair, walk, red (i.e. mainly nouns, verbs and adjectives), which are relatively easy to acquire. Content words are discussed in chapters 2 and 4.

It is suggested, therefore, that teachers might find it beneficial to concentrate on the activities described in chapters 5, 6 and 7 which discuss relational words. Content words are generally well catered for, sometimes incidentally, in the everyday activities of the infant school, when the child is frequently engaged in naming and describing. But there is no recommended division of time. Children's needs should govern where the emphasis is. Indeed, many may need considerable help over such a basic skill as listening which too often can be taken for granted.

Plan

Each chapter in this part of the book conforms to the same pattern. Specific aims associated with the skill in question are detailed. This is followed by a list of activities, including games, and, finally, by a consideration of the materials necessary to undertake the activities successfully.

Chapter 1　　　　Listening　　　　(Language skill 1)

Many disadvantaged children live in overcrowded home conditions where there is a great deal of noise—a confusion of sounds from television, radio, people and traffic. They have little opportunity to listen selectively and to develop the listening skills which are important in acquiring and developing language. The disadvantaged child tends to switch off and subsequently shows little inclination to listen to spoken language in the classroom. The instructions and guidance of the teacher, for example, may be disregarded or only partially attended to.

Aims

The important aim is to increase the child's motivation towards listening carefully and selectively. In responding to a variety of sounds in the classroom, the child has to learn to attend to some sounds and to disregard others. In the infant school, where children move freely among a variety of activities, it is particularly important for the child to be able to discriminate the relevant from the irrelevant. Systematic practice in discriminating sounds provides a basis for the more complex listening skills involved in dealing with spoken language.

The following suggestions relating to activities and materials are designed to encourage children to listen attentively to a variety of familiar sounds.

Activities/listening games

The following listening games can be played using familiar materials such as those listed on p. 15.

Recognition of everyday sounds (group game)

A variety of interesting sounds can be produced by tapping or moving familiar objects such as an empty glass, a piece of paper or a small bell (see p. 15 for a list of examples). Materials like these are shown to a group of children. The teacher (or later, the child) produces a sound (e.g. taps the glass or crumples the paper) while one child in the group wears a blindfold or faces away from the apparatus. The blindfold is removed, and he tries to identify the apparatus and repeat the sound. During the early stages the reticent child may do this simply by repeating the action. Later he will be encouraged to use the appropriate words such as:

'She knocked (tapped) the glass.'
'She rang the bell.'

The children can take it in turns both to produce and to identify the sounds.

This type of game should be extended to cover a wider exploration of everyday sounds such as: sounds in town, sounds in the park, sounds in my home, sounds of the sea or water, my favourite sounds, etc., which can stimulate discussion and the painting and collecting of pictures associated with sounds.

Recognition of everyday sounds (screen game)

Children too often communicate with one another simply by pointing and gesturing. A small cardboard screen placed across the middle of a table between two children seated opposite each other (see illustration on p. 44) prevents them from seeing each other and is, therefore, a very effective device for encouraging communication by talking. (Another useful device for encouraging children to communicate by talking is a battery-operated toy telephone. One child can phone messages and instructions to another child at the other side of the room, or in the adjacent room.)

One child has a small selection of sound effects materials such as an empty glass, a piece of paper or a small bell. He creates a sound with one of the materials and the child on the other side of the screen (who, of course, cannot see what has been done) tries to name the object and the action:

'You poured water.'

'You crumpled the paper.'

Alternatively, the second child could try to match the sound using his or her own set of materials, which are identical to the first child's collection.

Sorting sounds

A collection of 'shakers', for example pairs of matchboxes or plastic liquid soap containers containing materials such as sand, a few small pebbles, paper clips, etc. (see p. 15 for a list of examples), can be used by a child working singly in order to group sounds. He tries to sort the boxes into identical pairs or groups on the basis of the sound produced when each box is shaken. A coloured emblem underneath each box is useful as a checking device after the sorting has taken place.

Musical instruments

Familiar classroom musical instruments, such as the recorder, chime box, xylophone, triangle and auto harp can be used as a further extension of games with sounds. Musical instruments offer wide scope in exploring sounds and the basic actions (blowing, plucking and tapping) necessary to produce the sounds.

Cassette recorder

The cassette recorder has considerable potential in this field to encourage further experiments in games for creating and identifying sounds.

For example, everyday sounds such as a dog bark, a car engine running, children talking, footsteps, can be recorded and possibly augmented by commercially produced materials (see p. 15 for addresses).

The cassette recorder can be used to play a variety of sounds, while the children using language lotto or bingo cards (see p. 46 for description of lotto) can identify and cover the pictures associated with the sounds. Thus, the picture of a dog is covered at the sound of a dog barking, a car—engine noise, a tap—rushing water, a man walking—footsteps, and so on.

The use of the cassette recorder and a reference to further sources of materials are contained in more detail on pages 67 to 71.

The teacher's voice

The teacher's active participation in games cannot be overstressed. Any game or activity which concentrates on children listening to one voice can also be used frequently and with great effect. For example, tell a short story to a group of children. Then tell it a second time stopping before the end and asking one child to finish it. It is necessary to tell it all first as the child may either 'dry up' or finish it at random. After a few such games, and provided that the story is kept very short and simple, children will listen more and more carefully in case they should have to complete it.

Play Chinese whispers, with a small circle of children. The teacher whispers something to the first child such as 'It's very hot today', the next person whispers it to the neighbour and so on. The message is often quite different at the end, but as they get used to the game the children will listen more acutely to try to circulate the right message.

Materials

Common sound producing materials

The following sound sources can be used for some of the games described: 1 crumpling a piece of paper, 2 tearing paper, 3 ringing a bell, 4 tapping a gong (or small metal bar suspended by string), 5 footsteps, 6 plucking a taut string or rubber band, 7 pouring grains of sand onto paper, 8 tapping a glass containing a little water, 9 tapping a plastic cup, 10 tapping a wooden block, 11 pouring water from one cup into another, and 12 running a pencil across fluted cardboard.

Many variations in these sounds can be introduced by modifying the materials or actions: e.g. in (1) using cellophane paper; (2) tearing an old cloth; (6) varying the tautness of the string; (7) pouring small pebbles; (8) varying the level of the water; and so on.

'Shakers'

A set of more permanent sound-producing materials can be made from a collection of identical plastic containers or boxes. Pairs of these boxes, containing the same material such as a few dried peas, grains of sand, etc., can·be used as a set of shakers for sorting sounds. Boxes could contain the following: dried peas, grains of sand, small pieces of tinfoil, a small pebble, a small jingle-bell (taped to the inside of the box), and a small metal ball (ball-bearing).

The materials should be approximately equal in weight, as differences in weight would provide irrelevant clues (the child might match for weight rather than sound).

Tape-recorded material

Sound effects. A collection of recordings of familiar sounds of cars, dogs, people, etc., can be augmented with commercially produced sound effects. These are available on the following labels: E.M.I. Records 'EFX' series (obtainable from local record dealers or local library record lending services) and B.B.C. Radio Enterprises (from Broadcasting House, London W1A 1AA).

Sound lotto and stories in sound. A sound lotto game (similar to that described previously) in which recorded sounds cue the selection of pictures can be obtained from The Remedial Supply Co., Dixon Street, Wolverhampton. This company has also produced a series of 'Stories in Sound'—a number of sound effects such as a crash, running feet, telephone and ambulance klaxon linked to make up a story.

Chapter 2   Naming   (Language skill 2)

We now focus on the child's spoken language, starting with basic concrete vocabulary, the names of common objects such as chair, ball and box, common actions such as walking, eating and talking, and some basic sentence patterns.

Aims
Vocabulary
It cannot be taken for granted that the disadvantaged child understands or uses even the most obvious words. He often relies on pointing instead of naming. A minimal aim is that the child should acquire the basic concrete vocabulary of any immediate interests and surroundings. The nature of this vocabulary will depend largely on the materials in the various work areas and the activities associated with them. Here are a few examples:

Sand tray: objects—trough, sand, cup, scoop
                  actions—digging, pouring, scooping, sifting
Buildings: objects—blocks, bricks, wall, bridge
                  actions—building, making, holding, hammering
Home corner: objects—chair, bed, shelf, cup
                  actions—sitting, cleaning, dressing, pouring.

These examples merely hint at the many possibilities available (see part 2 for some lists of materials in work areas). Materials vary from one classroom to the next. It is impossible to cover adequately all the words used in and around the classroom. It is practical, though, to concentrate initially on the main objects and actions in particular classrooms, especially those items which interest the child.

Another aim of some of the activities outlined in this chapter is to encourage an understanding of a number of individual words which form the basis of common categories. For example, dog, cat, horse, mouse, belong to the category animal; shirt, dress, socks, hat, belong to the category clothes; man, woman, boy, girl, belong to the category people, and so on. (Categories are covered more fully in chapter 3.)

Language patterns
Some sequences of words occur frequently in our language and they form regularly used language patterns. Here are some basic examples:

Here's a car. ⎫
Here is a car. ⎪
There's a car. ⎬ statements
It's a car. ⎪
It's not a car. ⎭

Is it a car? ⎫
Isn't it a car? ⎬ questions
Isn't this/that a car? ⎭

An additional aim of the following activities is to facilitate the use of these patterns, which can be expanded and elaborated as the child's competence in the various language skills increases.

Activities

When young children encounter new materials for the first time, an initial period of free play is usually necessary to allow them to become familiar with these. They have to explore through seeing, touching, manipulating and sometimes by using the senses of taste and smell. This exploratory period should be accompanied by questions and statements relating to the children's play, the teacher encouraging them to talk about their activities. New and unfamiliar words relating to a particular centre of interest can be introduced during the discussion.

The following well-known games and activities can be used as a basis from which the teacher can select, adapting and extending them to suit the needs of the children.

Sorting

Children can be asked to sort a mixture of objects and pictures of objects into common groups which have the same name, such as: car, doll, block, dress, chair, etc. Children can be helped to realise that a word (label) such as car does not apply to one particular car, but a variety of cars which are different in colour, size and shape. Moreover, the car may be an object or a picture of an object (or some other form of representation such as a toy or model). Similarly there are many chairs of different colour, size and design, but they all share the label chair. Activities such as collecting or sorting a number of common objects (and pictures of objects) such as cars, blocks, dolls, pebbles, beads, etc., help strengthen this idea. The objects and pictures in a given collection share one name. While a child is picking out all the cars from a mixture of objects, those which are excluded can be termed 'not a car'. The use of the negative in this way helps to emphasize the idea of exclusion ('is a car'—inclusion; 'is not a car'—exclusion).

Sorting is a well-known classroom activity with many functions, some of which are discussed in chapters 3 and 4. Objects can be sorted according to criteria such as name (cars), colour (red), shape (squares), category (animals) and so on. It is important that materials used for sorting are carefully selected. Initially, only a small number should be used to avoid confusion. At a later stage, children can be introduced to the idea that a given collection of materials can be sorted according to changing criteria: according to name (cars, lorries, dresses, shirts), according to colour (reds, blues, browns), according to category (animals, clothes), and so on.

Kim's game

Naming the missing objects. A card version of this game is described on p. 45.

A few familiar objects such as a car, a doll and a block are placed on the table. The child is allowed a few moments to look at the objects and he is told that one will be taken away. He must then try to name the missing one. After a few moments he turns his back while one object is removed and the remaining objects are rearranged. He then looks at the remaining objects and tries to name the missing one. It is then replaced so that he can see if he is correct. Children can take it in turns to name and hide objects. In Kim's game naming the missing object and then seeing it revealed help to underline the idea that a word (symbol) stands for an object.

Surprise box (recognising objects by touch and feel)

The child is given a box containing several objects such as a rubber ball, a block, a toy dog and a small doll. She cannot see these objects, but places her hand through a hole (or curtain) in the box and tries to identify each object by touch and feel only. The game can be made more difficult by using pairs or groups of objects which are similar in shape: a coin, a wheel, a car, a lorry, a block, a box, a die, a cup, a jug, and so on.

What or who is it? (oral guessing game)

In this game simple definitions are given and the child tries to name the object (or objects, if there are several possibilities).

Examples:

We sleep on it . . .   She looks after sick people . . .
We kick it . . .   He brings the milk . . .
It has wheels . . .
It flies . . .

What am I doing? (children or puppets mime actions)

Here one child in a group mimes a simple action such as jumping, eating, crying or digging. Another child names the action and in turn mimes another action, another child names it and so on. The game becomes more difficult when several actions are mimed in sequence. In this way a short story can be created.

Language lotto (This game is described in more detail on p. 46 and illustrated on p. 47)

Usually four to six players are involved. Each player has a baseboard containing four pictures of various objects or actions. The leader who has a set of single cards, identical to those on the baseboards, holds up one of them. A player with a similar picture on the baseboard has to name it, saying, for example, 'It's a dog', in order to cover up his picture with a blank card. The game is completed when all the pictures on the baseboard are covered. This game gives the child practice in naming objects and actions using basic language patterns in the form of statements and questions. Variation in the patterns can be suggested by the teacher.

Naming sounds (using a screen)

This screen game, also described on p. 44, can be used to encourage the naming of objects and actions. Two children are seated at opposite ends of a table. A screen is placed between them so they cannot see each other. One child creates a sound—taps a glass, tears a piece of paper, rings a bell—and the other child names the material and action.

The following games are useful in drawing attention to component sounds of words. Awareness of the sounds which make up words has important implications for reading.

I spy

The leader pronounces the first sound or sounds, e.g. 'b' of a familiar word. The others try to guess by naming a number of words such as block, ball, boy, until they guess correctly. Similarly, rhyming words can be used. A starter such as 'hat' can lead to guesses such as cat, mat, rat, etc.

Which picture?

Several pairs of pictures of objects which have similar sounding names must be identified (e.g. in a language lotto game, previously described). Examples of similar sounding pairs and groups include: pig/peg, log/leg, dog/dig, foot/feet, car/cart/cat.

Songs and rhymes

There are many well-known songs and rhymes which help children to learn new words and to become familiar with language patterns. In addition, songs and rhymes have great value in increasing the child's motivation. The familiar verse 'The house that Jack built', for example, contains many names and actions which are repeated several times. A shortened form of this can be useful as rhythm and repetition are important aids to learning (See chapter 3 for other examples.)

Chapter 3   Categorising   (Language skill 3)

As mentioned on p. 17 a specific word such as coat may be applied to a wide variety of objects which, although they look similar, are different in several respects (for example, in colour and size). A word which denotes a category (i.e. a group or class) such as clothes may be applied to an even wider variety of objects which differ in many respects, but which all have a common use or function. Thus coat, sock and hat are different in appearance but are all for putting on or for wearing.

The advantaged child, in observing and discussing common objects and routine activities at home, gradually becomes aware that there are certain patterns in the organisation of his surroundings. Although his home contains a great variety of objects, they are not haphazardly distributed, but arranged and grouped in certain parts of the home or used in association with each other. For example, various rooms have certain functions: some for sleeping and dressing, another for cooking, another for sitting and watching television and so on.

Within this broad system there are other patterns of organisation. Various objects are grouped according to use. This kind of classification in the home and the frequent explanations and appropriate use of category words by the parents help the child to understand and break down the complexity of the surroundings. By contrast, the pattern of organisation and grouping in the home of some disadvantaged children may be less apparent or almost entirely absent. Moreover the disadvantaged child may have little opportunity to hear the appropriate vocabulary through discussion with his parents. Lack of understanding of category words often results in the child either overgeneralising or being too specific. For example, he might refer to a group of clothes as things (vague overgeneralising) or coats (too specific—naming one item).

Aims

The main aim of the following activities is to help the child understand and use category words such as people, animals, clothes and food and to grasp some of the reasons for grouping various individual items and objects into categories.

The reasons for grouping are usually based initially on minimal definitions and uses such as 'you eat these', 'you wear these' and 'all these have four legs and a tail'. Explanations such as these are, of course, inadequate, but they can help to form a basis for the development of a fuller understanding of categories or concepts of this kind.

In addition to categories, themes or topics such as hospital, travel, beach/seaside and farm provide other criteria for grouping words. A theme such as hospital will join together associated ideas such as doctor, nurse, patient, bandage and medicine.

The following list of categories and themes, many of which are discussed in the school, can be developed by the teacher as she wishes:

Category	Individual items
people (also family)	man (dad), woman (mum), girl (daughter, sister), boy (brother, son)
clothes	coat, shirt, dress, shoes, hat
animals (also pets, farm animals, zoo/wild animals)	dog, cat, horse, rabbit, elephant
food (also fruit, vegetables)	bread, meat, potatoes, apple
vehicles (also traffic)	car, lorry, bus, scooter, bicycle
buildings	house, garage, shop, shed, (block of) flats

tools	hammer, saw, screwdriver, drill, pliers
musical instruments	piano, guitar, recorder, trumpet, xylophone, drum
weapons	gun, sword, knife, bow and arrow

Theme	*Individual items*
hospital	doctor, nurse, patient, bandage, medicine
shop	shopkeeper, counter, till, shelf, packets, tins
fire station	fireman, helmet, fire engine, ladder, hose, axe
sea/beach	sand, shells, pebbles, seaweed, fish, bucket, water
plants	grass, flowers, trees, bark, branch, stem, root, soil
circus	tent, clown, acrobat, trapeze, animals
travel/transport	car, bus, train, road, rail, aeroplane, ship

The negative

An important aspect of categorising is the use of the negative (not) to denote exclusion from a category. For example, if the child is sorting animals into a group, an item which does not belong, such as a car, can be referred to as 'not an animal' in this context.

Activities

Work areas

The language associated with various work areas such as building, cooking, dressing-up and the home corner can help the child to understand the reasons for grouping different individual items according to categories. In building, for example, the category word building is associated with words such as house, garage, bricks, wall, window and roof. The home corner is particularly useful as it can be adapted to help develop a number of categories or themes such as home, hospital, cooking, tea-party and shop. The rooms of an open doll's house can be used for sorting various items into categories such as family, clothes, furniture and food.

The procedures of selecting and preparing materials to play with, putting away and tidying up afterwards are themselves useful sorting activities in which the child includes some objects and excludes others. The associated language, the naming of items and discussion of what they have in common, can help the child develop an understanding of the concepts.

Sorting

Sorting is a well-known activity which involves the grouping of a mixture of individual items into categories such as animals, clothes and people. Before the child can practise sorting, one or two underlying reasons, such as similarity in appearance or use, for grouping things together must be understood. The teacher using a small number of toys, or pictures such as a car, cat, lorry, and dog can draw attention to one or two features or uses that each pair have in common. As the child grasps the idea, other items such as a bus, horse and bicycle can be included.

The child can be misled if he relies only on the appearance of items when grouping. Food, for example, is a category made up of items which are very different in appearance. (For an example of a sorting game, see p. 57.)

Display table

The purpose of a display table is much the same as that of sorting. A display table or corner at a focal point in the classroom or corridor can be used for collections of objects which make up a particular category or theme. If, for example, the theme is plants, the children are encouraged to add to a collection on the display table by bringing objects such as flowers, grass, branches, leaves and roots. The display should not become too cluttered and should be changed after a week or two for a new theme.

Lotto (described on p. 46)
This game involves collecting and naming individual items such as dog, cat, horse, etc. Each game is arranged so that the items make up a category. Thus, there is animal lotto, clothes lotto, musical lotto, etc.

Variation of sorting (described in more detail on p. 56)
This game also involves the collection of individual items to make up categories. In most cases the category card contains a few examples of individual items and the child has to recognise items other than those illustrated on the category card.

Materials
Most of the materials needed for the games listed previously are readily available or easily improvised. Collections for display areas and sorting boxes can be brought by the children themselves.

Chapter 4   Describing   (Language skill 4)

The disadvantaged child may not understand or use many of those descriptive words or adjectives (of colour, size, texture, etc.) which denote qualities and features of objects. Similarly adverbs (such as quickly, slowly, quietly, etc.) which distinguish between actions may not be used or understood.

Aims

The main aims of the following activities are to encourage the child to discern differences in quality and type amongst a variety of objects and actions, using appropriate words which express these differences, and thereby expanding and extending language.

Here are some examples of descriptive vocabulary and common language patterns.

Adjectives include:
colours and shades (light/dark) of colour
shape—round, square, flat, straight, crooked, etc.
size—big, small, long, short, thick, thin, etc. (and comparatives—bigger, smaller, etc.)
texture—soft, hard, rough, smooth, etc. (and comparatives—softer, harder, etc.)
material—wood, plastic, glass, rubber, iron (metal), etc.
miscellaneous—wet, dry, heavy, light, new, old, etc. (and comparatives where appropriate)

Adverbs:
quickly, slowly, quietly, loudly, noisily, softly, gently, roughly, carefully, tightly, loosely

Language patterns
The big red block
The doll is (wearing) the blue dress
The man (who is) painting the wall
Tied the string tightly.

The understanding and use of concepts of 'same' and 'different' are crucial to this and many other aspects of language.

Activities

The introduction of adjectives can follow much the same procedure as that outlined in chapter 2: through questions and discussion relating to on-going activities. There is considerable overlap between naming and describing. As the child's descriptive skills are developed attention is drawn to the various qualities of materials such as colour, shape, texture and size.

The following areas and activities are particularly useful in this context:
Art—colours, shapes and patterns in painting
Dressing—colours and size (big, small, long, short, wide, etc.) of clothes
Building—size and shape of blocks, size and shape of buildings, type of material (plastic, wood, etc.) used
Nature table—colour and texture of objects such as wood, bark, fur, shell, acorn.

The following games are useful for encouraging the use of descriptive words.

Identikit

In the following two identikit games, two children, seated at opposite ends of a table, are separated from each other's view by a small screen placed across the middle of the table.

Description of clothing. One child has several dolls or pictures of people dressed in different clothes. He chooses one and describes the clothes in detail:

'He is wearing a brown hat . . . blue coat, a long blue coat . . . black trousers . . . carrying a stick . . .'

The child opposite, who cannot see the doll and therefore has to rely on the verbal description (he is, of course, encouraged to ask his partner questions), selects the appropriate clothes and places these on the doll or cut-out figure. In this example he has several hats, coats, trousers, etc., to choose from. These clothes can be made of cloth or coloured paper cut-outs.

When the two children think that their dolls match, they compare their dolls to see how accurately they have matched them. It is important that this game is regarded as one of co-operation between the children, and not a competition. If any points or tokens are awarded, these go to both partners. (See identikit clothes, p. 52.)

Description of face. One child has a number of pictures of different faces. He selects one face and describes the features in detail to his partner, 'Black hair . . . blue eyes, with glasses . . . no beard'. The partner on the other side of the screen has to make an 'identikit' face according to the description. He has a number of cut-out parts of the face (these are strips of cardboard cut horizontally)—a selection of, for example, black and yellow or fair hair, pairs of blue eyes and brown eyes, glasses (see identikit face, p. 54).

Drama

Variations of the identikit games can be played in group or class situations where, for example, instead of using dolls or identikit clothes or faces, the children act the parts of policeman, witness, robber and victim in a play about a robbery or an accident. Police ask questions and witnesses describe people involved so that they can be identified.

Sorting

In order to develop the concepts underlying descriptive words, objects are sorted into groups according to colour, shape, size, etc. The use of the negative is important. Things which don't belong to a given group, say of round objects, can be referred to as 'not round'.

Display table

The purpose of this is much the same as in sorting. A display table or corner at a focal point in the classroom or corridor is used for collections of objects. If, for example, the focus word is 'round', a coin, plate and saucer are placed on the table, and the children are encouraged to bring objects which are round to add to the collection. It is important that displays are changed after a few days. Collections should not become too cluttered. The display table is useful for collections of objects which have a definite texture such as rough, smooth, hard and soft; for colours, and shades of colours, e.g. dark red and light red.

Some of the activities and games, already outlined in chapter 2, are, with certain modifications, appropriate for encouraging descriptive words. For example:

Kim's game. A number of blocks of different colours are used. One is removed and the child tries to name the missing colour. Similarly, one of a number of shapes (cardboard cut-outs, which can be round, square, star, zig-zag, etc.) is removed and the child names the missing one.

Surprise box. Instead of naming the hidden objects, they are described in terms of shape and texture.

Language lotto. The object of each set of lotto cards is the same, but they vary in colour, size and shape. For example, on each card of a given set is a picture of a man, but each man has different clothes. (See lotto game 'What's he/she wearing?', p. 50.)

The introduction of adverbs, that is descriptive words relating to actions, can be linked with physical games, music-and-movement and drama, especially mime, and other activities involving bodily movements.

In order to focus on differences between actions a familiar action can be repeated in several ways. One child demonstrates an action, another describes it using the appropriate adverb and then mimes it in a different way, a third child describes, then mimes, and so on. Examples of actions and variations include:

clapping hands—softly, loudly, slowly, quickly
walking—softly, loudly, slowly, quickly, happily, sadly
talking—quietly, loudly, slowly, quickly, happily, sadly
sleeping—quietly, noisily, restlessly, peacefully
opening/tying a parcel—carefully, carelessly, slowly, quickly
stroking a cat—gently, carefully, slowly.

Children can take turns in miming and describing (using the appropriate adverbs) the characteristic movement of:

an old man walking, a puppy playing, a tortoise walking, a hungry dog eating, a thirsty child drinking, a child taking medicine, a snake moving, a big bird/small bird flying.

During story-telling children can take turns to mime the movements of characters in the story. They can rehearse the various actions first, and while the story is being told the actions are cued in.

Chapter 5   Denoting position   (Language skill 5)

An object's position in relation to its surroundings is denoted by words such as on, under and between. Words of this type can cause difficulty because they are relative terms and are used in many different and changing situations.

Consider, for example, the phrases:

under the table
under the shoe
under the mat.

In each case the word under is associated with positions which (from the observer's vantage point) are relatively low down or near the floor. This can be misleading as under also refers to positions which are relatively high up such as:

under the shelf (the shelf is high above the observer's head)
under the roof
under the light.

Another possible cause of confusion is the fact that there are several ways of denoting an object's position in relation to its surroundings. For example, the doll is on the table but it is also between the box and the book, and in the room.

(Incidentally words such as in, up and on do not always refer to positions in space. Consider, for example, expressions such as 'Be there in a moment', 'What's he up to?' and 'On no account must you'.)

Aims

The aims of the following activities are to enable the child to understand and use a relatively small number of relational words of position. These provide the child with a framework for organising and describing complex and changing physical surroundings. Wherever an object is placed the child should be able to denote the relationship of the object to its surroundings.

Here, in three main groups, are a number of frequently used relational words of position:

(a) object's position in relation to its surroundings—on, in, under, next to, in front of, behind, between, near, far
(b) part of an object or area—middle, corner, edge, side, top, bottom, front, back, inside, left (side), right (side)
(c) direction of movement of an object—up, down, around, through, forwards, back-wards, sideways, over, into.

Note. The above three groups of 'position' words are not mutually exclusive, as some words can appear in more than one group. For example, 'around' not only indicates movement, it can also refer to position or placement.

Similar basic sentence patterns to those used in chapters 2 and 4 can be encouraged:

Where's the ball?
The ball is in the box.
Put it between the box and . . .

Activities

Words denoting position and positional relationships are frequently used in many class-room and work area activities:

Put the blocks in the box.
Where's the book? On the shelf.
It fell down. Pick it up.
Put the plate in the middle of the table . . . the spoon near the edge.
The mouse is hiding under the straw in the corner of the cage.

Physical games, music and movement
Games in which the child is physically involved are particularly useful for developing an understanding of position words:

Jump over the box . . . through the hoop . . . run around the chair . . . crawl under the table.

Demonstrations
In order to clarify important position words, a few simple materials such as a ball, cup and table can be used to provide an uncluttered demonstration. Thus, for example, the child can be asked whether the ball is: in the cup, behind the cup, under the table, on the corner of the table. Alternatively, the child is asked to place the ball appropriately when given instruction.

A scene or flannelgraph can be made with a small number of flannel cut-outs, such as a hill, a tree, a fence and gate. These are arranged on the flannelgraph and a character such as a rabbit can be made to: run up the hill . . . over the fence . . . through the gate . . . around the tree.

Children can take turns to give and carry out instructions.

Building game (using a screen)
Two children seated at opposite ends of a table are separated from each other's view by a small screen placed across the middle of the table. One child has a number of diagrams or actual models of towers, bridges, trains and houses made of blocks, cotton reels, matchboxes, cardboard, corks and other common materials. She instructs her partner, who cannot see the model, how to build, say, a bridge using a similar set of materials:

'Put a cotton reel on the yellow block . . . another cotton reel on the red block . . . a piece of cardboard across the cotton reels . . . a car under the bridge.'

Questions can be asked during the building and when both partners think that their models match they compare them.

Note. Since many young children cannot distinguish between left and right, it helps if each player wears a tag or band on the right wrist. (See Building game, p. 58 for further examples.)

Scene or plan (using a screen)
The situation is the same as that described above. Each child has a three-dimensional model (made of boxes and cardboard) or plan on a sheet of paper of a town or farm. Each child has an identical set of toys—car, lorry, dog, man, woman. One child places a toy in a given area on his plan and instructs the partner to do likewise:

'Put the dog near the tree . . . the car between the house and the garage . . . the man in the house . . .'

Language lotto (bingo)
In this game the procedure is the same as for language lotto described in chapters 2, 4, etc. The lotto cards consist of pictures of a cup in various positions in relation to a box and a table. The child has to describe the position of the cup before covering up the picture.

'The cup is in the box.'

'The cup is under the table.'

(See 'Where's the cup?' lotto, p. 60.)

Chapter 6   Sequencing   (Language skill 6)

The ability to organise events verbally in sequence is of great importance in communicating stories, instructions, daily events, news and other narratives. Some important aspects of sequencing events include:
   understanding and using 'linking' words of time such as then, before, after, while;
   understanding and using sequence words such as first, next;
   understanding and using words denoting broad time slots such as morning, afternoon, day(time), today, tomorrow;
   understanding and using a variety of tenses.
Many children have the benefit of hearing, through conversation with their parents, language which is directly associated with daily routine such as getting up, washing, dressing, eating and going to schoool:
Wash before you get dressed.
No, put your shoes on after your socks.
Eat your breakfast while I . . .
Can do that later, but first . . .
We'll do that tomorrow morning.
Not only do daily events such as these follow an orderly pattern, but the key relational words of time are used frequently in a variety of situations. This type of experience enables the child to use these key relational words in a variety of other situations which involve sequencing events.
   For another child on the other hand, not only is the daily routine at home less orderly, but he also lacks the benefit of hearing systematic language patterns associated with these events. It is, therefore, not surprising that he has poorly developed ideas of sequence, order and duration of time.

Aims
The main aims of the following activities are to enable the child to understand and use some key relational words of time in a variety of sequencing situations. Here are some examples of key words:
   words which link events—then, before, after, when, while;
   words which denote order of events and amount of time—first, next, last, soon, now, later, until;
   words which denote time slots—morning, afternoon, day(time), night(time), today, yesterday, tomorrow.
Note. The above three groups of the words are not exclusive as some words can appear in more than one group. For example, 'now' and 'later' also refer to time slots.
   It is also important to encourage the use of a variety of relational words of time rather than the repetitive use of 'and then'. The following examples illustrate some language patterns involving relational words of time:
(a) (first) catch the ball then run to . . .
    (simple chaining—events linked by 'then')
(b) catch the ball before you run to . . .
    ('Before' emphasises that one event must precede another.)
(c) dry the cups after you have washed them.

27

(The use of the linking word 'after' implies that the order of events in this particular sentence pattern is a reversal of the order of events which actually takes place.)

(d) bring me the paintbrush when you have finished.

('When' fulfils a function similar to 'after'.)

(e) you build a tower while she makes . . .

('While' indicates that the two actions 'building' and 'making' take place at the same time.)

Note. Events are also linked by connectives such as but, if, so and because.

Examples:

He fell but he wasn't hurt . . .

It will break if you . . .

Closed the door so (that) the cat . . .

The use of these connectives is discussed in chapter 7.

Other activities should help the child master the various verb changes which are closely associated with sequence and carry important differences in meaning. Consider the loss of meaning if a child fails to use (or fails to hear) appropriate changes in a verb: He run away . . . (The meaning is not clear.)

The following patterns indicate some important types of verb changes which enable the child to express when (past, present or future) an event takes place:

He is running away.

He has run away.

He ran away.

He is going to run away.

He might run away.

He runs away.

Activities

There are many activities in the school (in work areas, classroom and general school routine) which present opportunities for drawing attention to relational words of time. Questions and statements referring to the time relations between events can be made by focusing on linking words such as before, after, when, and while.

Work areas

The following examples suggest broad sequences of events, commonly occurring in the classroom:

Home Corner—laying the table, serving food, washing up

Cooking—mixing, baking, eating

Craft—cutting, glueing, painting

Building—build walls, windows, roof

Art—clipping paper on easel, mixing powder and water, painting, hanging picture.

School routine

Children gradually become aware that there is a general routine of activities and that they occupy certain time slots during the day. The following examples of activities in the school show how events can be related to each other in time:

First we take off our coats then go to our classroom.

Listen to the radio after play-time.

Wash our hands before dinner(time).

Go home after story-time.

(Notice the words 'play-time', 'story-time', 'dinner-time'—events which occupy regular time slots in the day.)

Examples of broader time slots are:

We went to the fire station yesterday.

The painter is coming tomorrow to . . .

(Notice the use of 'is' with the present participle to imply future intention.)

It's raining today.

The teacher can use examples such as these to discuss with the child various aspects of time relevant to situations in which he or she is involved, focusing on key time words.

Action sequences (using pictures or mime)

In order to highlight the importance of key words associated with time sequences, sets of three or four pictures (or, where possible, mimed actions by children or puppets) depicting a number of events in sequence can be used for discussion. The following example illustrates how a sequence can be used to focus on key aspects of time.

Sequence of events

Pictures of: 1 girl looking at ball on top of cupboard, 2 girl standing on box reaching for ball on cupboard, 3 girl with ball in hand, standing on floor.

(See note on materials, p. 30 for further examples of pictures in sequence.)

Discussion relating to this sequence can be encouraged by questions relating to each action individually:

What's happening here (in this picture)?

What is she doing?

Questions relating to events:

Which picture shows she is reaching for the ball?

Which picture shows she is going to get the ball?

Which picture shows she has taken the ball down?

Questions relating to events which take place before or after one another:

Where was she (what was she doing) before she climbed the box?

Where was she (what was she doing) after she'd reached the ball?

Why did she stand on the box?

Story-telling (using this sequence)

The same pictures as used above can then be scrambled. The child is asked to rearrange them in order and tell a short story about them.

This method of using a few pictures in sequence can be used as a basis for longer stories. The child is then encouraged to attempt longer sequences and to rely less on the supporting pictures. Here is an example of a more difficult series of pictures where events are less obviously linked and which require more language to relate the events to each other: 1 boy playing with matches, 2 room on fire, 3 telephone, 4 fire brigade.

'Tell the story' game

This game involves the collection of cards which make up a sequence of events (a story). The story might involve the taking the ball from the cupboard sequence, mentioned previously.

Each player is given one large theme card which shows the girl, ball, cupboard and box drawn as individual items showing no connection with each other. The three smaller cards are as described previously. Each other player has a large theme card and three smaller sequence cards. All the smaller sequence cards are shuffled and placed in a pile between the players. Each player takes it in turn to pick up a card, keep it if it belongs to the sequence (checks this by looking at the theme card), or place it under the pile if it does not. If it is kept the action depicted is described. When all three which make up the set have been acquired, he or she places them on the table in sequence and tells the story. (See 'Tell the Story' game on p. 62.)

Materials

Picture sequences can consist of simple drawings sketched on individual cards, depicting different actions ('pin men' are often adequate for this purpose). Cartoon strips, taken from children's comics, can be cut into individual pictures and pasted on separate cards.

Here are some examples of sequences which can be used in the activities already described.

1. ball on roof   2. girl climbs up ladder   3. girl retrieves ball
1. dog chases cat   2. cat climbs tree   3. dog tries to climb tree
1. lighted match falls   2. flames spread   3. fire brigade
1. rabbit in cage   2. door is opened   3. rabbit gets out
1. rabbit in cage   2. hops towards lettuce   3. eats lettuce
1. builder lays bricks   2. puts in windows   3. builds roof
1. cars approach each other   2. crash   3. ambulance and stretcher
1. man snatches bag   2. police chase man   3. man arrested
1. man puts on coat   2. takes umbrella   3. goes outside with umbrella up.

Useful ideas for sequences can be obtained from various pre-readers. Sets of sequence cards are contained in *Look and find a story* published by E. J. Arnold.

Chapter 7   Reasoning   (Language skill 7)

The term reasoning refers broadly to the use of language for planning, predicting (antici-pating) and solving problems. These functions often involve the use of relational words such as if, because and but which relate a cause to an effect or condition.

Planning, predicting, problem-solving

The advantaged child is accustomed to using language to plan his activities and to think about problems. He will often talk to himself (aloud or sub-vocally) before and during an activity. In this way he can use language to discuss plans and intentions, consider several alternative courses of action and make decisions before carrying out actions.

This is a crucial area of language usage as it enables the child to play and explore systematically and purposefully, guided by his own language. Disadvantaged children, on the other hand, are often not accustomed to using language to plan and anticipate events. They may play in a haphazard and unsystematic manner. Without an overall verbal plan, play and exploration tend to be desultory, and one action is unrelated to another.

Another important aspect of the advantaged child's language is his constant question-ing. He frequently demands to know why certain things happen and is constantly searching for cause. By contrast the disadvantaged child may not appear to have the same curiosity and questioning attitude or the ability to ask questions purposefully and systematically.

Aims

The main aim is to encourage the disadvantaged child to use language to plan activities and talk about his intentions before actually carrying them out. In making a simple pre-diction—'It will fall'—or a plan—'I'll put the block on the box'—he is recalling previous play experiences with similar materials and relating these present circumstances so that he can anticipate what is likely to happen and plan accordingly.

In encouraging the child to make a prediction or plan, it is important that he should put his statement to the test by carrying out the action. Of course, the action will not always accurately correspond to the statement but accuracy is less important than the actual verbal attempt to predict and plan. Predicting and planning involve the use of relational words such as if, because and but. The following are examples of language patterns commonly used in reasoning:

It will break if you drop it.
He is crying because he fell.
He closed the door so that the rabbit couldn't escape.
He hurt himself but he didn't cry.
It will fall unless you hold it.
He ate his dinner although he wasn't hungry.
You can either glue it on or tie it (also neither . . . nor).

Activities

Predicting

There are many situations which can be used to encourage the child to predict or anticipate an event or action. The following example illustrates this procedure.

The child (or teacher) holds a rubber ball above the table and he is asked what will happen if he lets the ball go. The child is encouraged to make a prediction (e.g., 'It will fall . . . bounce') before letting the ball go. Having carried out the action to see if it corresponds to the statement, he is then encouraged to make predictions using other familiar materials such as a block, a piece of paper, a tower of wooden blocks (removing lower block, 'It will fall'; removing top block, 'It won't fall'). The main aim of this kind of procedure is to give the child the opportunity of making a prediction and then putting it to the test. Language is translated into visible action. The accuracy of the prediction is not as important as actually attempting to predict.

As the child becomes familiar with the procedure, he can be encouraged to talk about several possibilities using relational words such as:

but ('It will fall but it won't bounce.')

unless ('It will fall over unless you hold it.')

Note. More difficult predictions involve recalling two separate sets of experiences and relating these to each other. Example: the child has seen a ball bouncing on various surfaces (but perhaps not on dry sand); he has seen a number of objects (but not a ball falling on dry sand). The child combines the knowledge gained from these experiences to predict (from several possibilities) what will happen when a ball is dropped on dry sand.

Some materials and situations which can be used to encourage predictions include:

Falling objects—rubber ball, wooden block, cork, marble, ball of plasticine, piece of paper, feather, teaspoon of sand, pastry cutters.

Predictions can be made comparing appropriate objects from the above examples, regarding:

How will they fall (e.g. straight down or glide)?

Will they bounce? How will they bounce? (e.g. high/low, straight up and down/to one side)

What sound (e.g. loud/soft) will they make on landing?

What mark will they make on different surfaces?

Will they change shape on landing?

Further variations can be introduced by changing the landing surface: e.g. soft cushion, wet/dry sand, uneven/sloping surface.

Moving objects—Moving a cloth over drops of water on a table (prediction about what will happen to the water and the cloth).

Moving a rubber over a pencil mark (prediction about what will happen to the mark and the rubber).

Moving a paintbrush over paper (prediction about the mark on the paper and the paint on the brush).

Moving one end of lever or see-saw downwards (prediction about movement of the other end).

Rolling a marble down two ramps—one steep slope, one gentle slope (prediction about which ramp will make the marble go further).

Slowly tipping a cup of water (prediction about where the water will go).

Taking away lower block (also upper block) of a tower made of wooden blocks (prediction about what will happen to the other blocks).

Floating/sinking objects and trough of water (predictions about whether they will float/sink; sink slowly/quickly).

Planning

A work area such as the sand tray gives the teacher the opportunity of encouraging the child to discuss and plan an activity before carrying it out. In doing this the child is recalling previous play experience with the materials and attempting to plan by naming the materials needed and describing what to do with them.

The following example illustrates this procedure: the child decides to build a castle in the sand. First, he is encouraged to name the materials he will need, e.g. wet sand, bucket, pebble, etc. He is then encouraged to describe his first step (for example, 'I'll put sand in the bucket') before he actually carries out this action. He continues to describe and carry out the various stages of the activity until the building is completed.

When the child becomes familiar with this procedure he is encouraged to describe several stages at a time before carrying them out. The eventual aim is that after considerable practice he should be able to describe an overall plan including a description of the finished object, names of materials and a description of the various stages from the beginning to the final outcome of an activity. This is a complex and difficult task; do not expect a child to be able to do it too soon.

It is important that planning is not approached as a rigid procedure. The child might wish to change his course of action. This should be encouraged but he should first describe his intention before doing so. Other work areas which can be used to encourage verbal planning include:

Building—naming 'junk' materials needed such as boxes, cardboard strips, cardboard rolls, coloured paper, blocks, string and glue; describing stages in building, for example: house, tower, train, man (robot), rocket

Cooking—naming ingredients and describing stages such as pouring, mixing, cooking, serving, eating

Laying the table—naming articles needed—cups, plates, spoons, chairs, etc., and describing how they are arranged

Dressing—naming clothes and describing the stages of dressing.

Sequencing and story telling

In attempting to plan the child relies to a large extent on the ability to sequence events. Picture sequences, such as those described on p. 30, can be used to help the child plan and anticipate. For example, the first two pictures of the sequence showing the dog chasing the cat can be discussed, and the child is then encouraged to anticipate the event(s) which may follow. The child is encouraged to suggest several means of escape for the cat: up a tree, into a house, or behind a fence. Story-telling in the wider sense can be used in a similar way. The child is told part of a story and at a given point he is encouraged to tell what he thinks might then happen. For example, the child is told a story in which a boy loses his dog. He is then asked, 'Where should the boy look?' 'Whom should he ask?' Again several possibilities should be discussed.

Problem-solving

Simple problems can either be presented in a practical situation, in picture form or in the form of a verbal statement. The child is encouraged to discuss various possibilities before carrying them out.

Practical situation/picture: a ball is placed on top of a tall cupboard and the child is asked how he or she can get it down. Suggestions such as:

Stand on a chair.
A stick to knock it down.
Shake the cupboard.

can be discussed before they are tested or discouraged. The ball is then replaced by a glass of water and again suggestions are discussed.

33

Statement: an everyday problem such as 'I'm feeling cold. What shall I do?' can be stated, and the child is encouraged to state several solutions such as:

Put on a coat.

Close the door.

Stand near the fire.

Other examples of statements include:

He has hurt his arm.

The doll's clothes are wet.

The wheel has come off the car. ..

The cat is running away from the dog.

The box is too heavy to lift.

The tower (blocks) keeps falling down.

It's dark in the room.

Some water has spilled on the floor.

(For each problem several 'solutions' should be encouraged.)

Language games

Language games such as Picture reading and Twenty questions can be used to help the child to discuss and predict.

Picture reading: A picture of a familiar scene, such as a doll's tea party, is covered with a large sheet of paper in which a small hole is cut. The hole reveals only a small part of the picture such as a cup, for example. The child is asked to name or describe other objects which might be in the picture. He is encouraged to suggest ideas (related to the cup), such as: saucers, other cups, plates and a table. The covering sheet of paper can be moved to reveal another part of the picture, encouraging the child to make further guesses, and change previous guesses if necessary.

As in other games and activities requiring predictions and guesses, the attempt at making the guess is more important than its accuracy.

Twenty questions: The modified version of Twenty questions described here is aimed at helping the child to ask questions to identify one object from a choice of several objects, by including some possibilities and excluding others. The following example illustrates the procedure: Two similar dolls, one dressed in yellow and one in green, are placed in front of the child. He is told to ask which one has a coin in its pocket. He must not point. If, for example, the child asks 'Is it the doll in yellow?' and the answer is 'No', then it must be the one in green. He checks to see that this is so. (The use of negative information in this way is an important principle of the game.)

This procedure is repeated several times, and in each case the child does not know which doll has the coin, and he asks only one question to identify it. (Instead of hiding the coin each time, the teacher can simply ask the child 'Which doll am I thinking about?') When the child is accustomed to the idea of the game, four dolls can be used: man in yellow, man in green, woman in yellow, woman in green. The child is encouraged to identify the one with the coin by asking only two questions, for example:

'Is it a man?'　　　　　　('No')

'Is she wearing green?'　　('No')

'It must be the woman in yellow.'

It is helpful in the early stages to cover up (or move to one side) the dolls which are eliminated. In the example above, when the child learns that it isn't a man, he can move both men to one side, and his next question refers to the colour of the women's clothes.

(For further suggestions see p. 64.)

PART 2

Work Areas: Environments
for exploration and discussion

Chapter 8   Work Areas

Introduction

In part 1 we discussed ways in which language development can be encouraged through various activities. We now turn to the use of specific work areas. Work areas such as sand, water, building, painting and home corner, in which the child plays and experiments with various materials, provide rich opportunities for the teacher to encourage the development of language skills through discussion, questions and explanations. Language which is linked meaningfully to the activities in which the child is engaged not only helps to develop important language skills and patterns, but also enables him to play and explore more purposefully and with increased interest.

In organising and equipping work areas it is important to provide a variety of topics of interest so that the child can explore and manipulate materials using important language skills in many different situations.

As mentioned in part 1, crucial language skills are learned through understanding and expressing relationships (e.g. of space, time, cause-effect) between objects, actions and ideas. Virtually any materials which interest and stimulate the child can be used to focus on these types of relationship and the appropriate language patterns. Since the range of possible approaches is so wide, it is important that the following chapter on work areas and materials is regarded only as an example which indicates the potential use of simple materials in fostering language development.

Plan

The one chapter in part 2 discusses how activities in two important work areas can be related to language development. The seven key skills identified in part 1 are outlined in detail in relation to the sand area and the home corner. The outline of activities in these areas provides a framework which can be adapted and applied to other work areas and materials. Part 2 concludes with examples of materials in two other work areas—water and building.

Language skills

The breakdown of language into seven skills follows the same approach as in part 1. It must be emphasised again that in practice each of the seven key skills is not covered in isolation and that, because of the unified nature of the spoken language, overlap between the skills is both inevitable and desirable. It should also be stressed that special attention should be focused on those language skills which express important relationships, namely denoting position, sequencing and reasoning.

Sand area

Materials

Materials commonly found in a sand area include:
  tray of dry sand, tray of wet sand, shells, pebbles; buckets (large, small), watering can,

funnels (small bore, large bore), sieves (fine, coarse), colander, moulds, pastry cutters, wide plastic tubing, cups and scoops (various sizes, made from liquid soap containers), spade, roller (rolling pin), rake, dowel rods, flags (coloured paper glued to rods); toys: lorry (tip-up), bulldozer, motor roller, crane, car, soldiers, builders, animals; storage· large containers (including bucket), shelves, hooks: brush and pan.

Damp sand can be moulded into many different forms and shapes: three-dimensional models of towers, ships, hills and hollows: two-dimensional drawings and shapes (using a finger or pointed rod), patterns and imprints of objects such as a sieve, funnel, pastry cutter, car (tracks), child's hand.

Dry sand can be used for scooping and pouring, filling containers with a scoop, pouring from one container into another (e.g. from a funnel into a narrow container); separating (by sifting) materials such as pebbles and shells from sand, or separating coarse grains of sand from fine grains: sprinkling, scattering grains of sand.

Activities

In order to maintain the focus on language the following activities commonly associated with the sand area are described in relation to the language skills discussed in part 1.

Listening

The teacher can draw attention to various sounds which can be created with some materials. By pouring dry sand on paper or shaking sand in a plastic cup, the child can be encouraged to create other sounds.

Children can practise recognizing sounds by playing a game in which one child creates a sound while another child looks the other way and then tries to repeat the sound. Later, instead of repeating the sound, the child tries to name the object and action involved.

You poured sand on paper.
You shook sand in a cup.
Here are some examples of 'sound effects' in the sand tray:
sprinkling dry sand on paper
shaking sand in a plastic cup (also pebbles, shells)
rubbing sand between the fingers
dropping a stone on wet sand
stirring sand in a cup
drawing a rod or pencil across wet sand
drawing a rod across a sieve, across a colander
tapping various objects such as a plastic mug, a shell, a stone, on the side of the sand tray.

Naming and describing

Through discussion the teacher can introduce the names of various materials and associated actions in the sand corner, concentrating on less familiar objects such as: funnel, sieve, mould, roller.

Relevant descriptive words might include:
shape—round, square, hollow, etc.
texture—fine, smooth, coarse, soft
size—wide, narrow, long
material—plastic, wood, metal
various colours.

Interest can then be focused on actions such as: digging, pouring, sifting, sprinkling.

The movement (flow) of sand can be observed and the child's attention can be drawn to relevant adverbs such as: slowly, quickly, gently, quietly.

Kim's game (variations of this game are described on pp. 17, 23 and 45). A few objects such as a shell, a pebble, a small cup and a flag are placed on a tray of dry sand. The child is allowed a few moments to look at the objects (naming them) and is told that one will be buried. He must then look at the remaining objects and try to name the hidden one. Having named it, he digs it out to see if he is correct. Children take it in turns to name and bury objects. The game can be made more difficult by increasing the number of objects.

Surprise box (a variation of this game is described on p. 17). Objects of contrasting shapes and patterns such as a funnel, sieve, shell and mould are placed in a large bucket under the table. The child tries to identify each object by touch and feel only, naming and describing it before taking it out of the bucket.

What is it? (oral guessing game—also described on p. 18). Simple descriptions and definitions are given and the child tries to name the object.
Examples:
    It is round, made of plastic and has holes in it.
    We use it to dig holes in the sand.
    We use it to fill the cup with sand.
    We use it to cut shapes in wet sand.
    We use it to sprinkle water on the sand (and flowers).
    We fill it with sand and the sand pours out of the other end.

Categorising

The use or function of various materials in the sand area can be discussed in the course of play and exploration. When the child becomes familiar with the various ways in which materials can be used, discussion can centre on grouping materials into categories such as *building*. The child can be asked to select from a number of materials (e.g. sand, bucket, pebbles, car, bulldozer, mould, lorry, tubing, funnel), those objects which are used for building (e.g. building a house). In choosing materials such as wet sand, bucket, pebbles, bulldozer and lorry, the function of each can be discussed with frequent reference to the category word building.

Other examples of categories (and individual items belonging to categories) in the sand area include:
    Vehicles—car, lorry, bulldozer
    People—builders, soldiers, farmer
    Things for pouring (dry sand)—scoop, funnel, tube, cup
    Things for shaping/moulding (damp sand)—moulds, pastry cutters, dowel rod, spade.

Denoting position

Discussions relating to the movement of sand (in pouring and modelling) and the position of objects in the sand tray can help the child to understand and use relational words which denote position.
Examples:
Movement of sand—
    Sand goes through the holes in the sieve.
    Sand runs (flows) through the tube into the bucket.
    Sand falls from high to low.
    Sand flows down the slope.
    Sand will spill over the edge.
Position of objects—
    The funnel is in a corner of the tray.
    Make a hill in the middle of the tray.
    Put a flag on top of the tower.
    The shell is hidden under the sand.

Here are two examples of games which can be used to focus on words which denote position.

Drive the car. This game can be played in damp sand. A landscape of hills, a tunnel, a bridge, interlinking roads, a house and garage, trees, flags, and so on can be used to focus on words which denote position. A child with a toy car is given instructions by the teacher (or another child) to drive her car to various parts of the area. Here are some examples of instructions:

Drive the car out of the garage . . . backwards towards the house . . . forwards towards the red flag . . . past the red flag . . . under the bridge . . . through the tunnel . . . around the hill . . . to the top of the hill . . . park between the yellow flag and the tree.

When the child becomes familiar with this kind of procedure and with the position words involved, the teacher can move the car to various parts of the area, asking the children where the car is at a number of identifiable points, encouraging the children to use words (they must not point) which denote position such as those used in the preceding instructions. Alternatively, the children can instruct the teacher or each other to move the car to various parts of the area.

Hunt the treasure. In this game a number of objects such as a funnel, shell, stone, car, tree and flag are placed on various parts of the sand area. A coin is hidden in the sand, and the child is told where to find it; the position of the treasure is described in relation to the objects on the sand.

Examples:

It is hidden in the middle of the tray.
It is under the shell.
It is between the shell and the stone.
It is in the corner where the funnel is.
It is behind the car.

Sequencing

In activities such as making models or buildings in the sand tray there is usually a distinct sequence of events. The child can be encouraged to give a verbal commentary while building, for example, a sand castle. Here is an example of a sequence commonly used:

Fill the bucket with sand . . . pack it down firmly . . . cover the top with something flat . . . turn the bucket upside down . . . tap the bucket and slowly lift it up.

The teacher can focus on relational words of time such as first, before and after, by asking questions such as:

What did you do first?
What did you do after you turned the bucket upside down?
What did you do after you tapped the bucket?

Drive the car. This game, consisting of the same type of landscape of hills, tunnel, bridge, trees, etc. (described on pages above), can be used to focus on important aspects of sequencing. The teacher asks the child to drive the car to various parts of the area, and then asks questions relating to the sequence of the journey.

Example:

Drive the car from the garage to the bridge . . . now drive it under the bridge . . . after you go past the tree, turn towards the hill and stop near the tunnel. See if the tunnel is clear before you drive through.

(Initially, of course, a shorter sequence would be used.)

The teacher then asks questions which focus on relational words of time, encouraging the child to answer verbally without pointing.

Examples:

Where was the car before it came to the tree?
Where did the car go after it went under the bridge?

38

Where did the car go after it went past the flag?

Further variations can be introduced by instructing two children to follow the direction simultaneously:

Drive the car around the hill while the lorry is being loaded with sand . . . keep driving until the lorry's full before you stop. Where was the car while the lorry was being loaded? When did the car stop?

Reasoning

The term reasoning refers to the use of language for predicting, planning and problem-solving. These functions often involve the use of relational words such as if, because, but, unless, which relate a cause to an effect or condition.

Predicting

The following example illustrates a procedure in which the child makes a verbal prediction and then puts it to the test: A wooden block is held about a foot above a mound of dry sand and the child is asked to state what he thinks will happen to the block, and to the mound of sand, if the block is released. Having made a prediction (e.g. that the block will fall and the mound will be flattened), the child carries out the action to test his statement.

Examples of materials/situations for encouraging predictions—

Falling objects:

Block, ball, cup, sieve, mould, pastry cutter, teaspoon of sand, rake. Predictions can be made comparing appropriate objects from the above examples, contrasting their impact on dry sand (usually soft landing, disturbing the surface) and wet sand (usually making an imprint).

Examples of questions for predictions include:

Will it bounce?

Will it make a loud/soft noise on landing?

Will it make a mark? What shape will the mark be?

Will the sand bridge collapse if you drop a stone, shell, or sand on to it?

The same procedure can be used for predicting the effect of moving objects:

Moving a dowel rod across the surface of damp sand (prediction about the mark it will make).

Driving a car on sand (prediction about the marks it will make).

Moving a toy rake across sand (prediction about the marks it will make).

Moving a cylindrical roller over an uneven area of sand (prediction about its effect on the sand).

Rolling a ball down a steep hill/a gently sloping hill (prediction about which slope will make it go further).

Putting dry sand/wet sand into similar funnels (prediction about flow of sand out of the funnel).

Filling two funnels (one wide bore, one narrow bore) with dry sand (prediction about rate of flow, and which will empty the sooner).

Planning

The sand area provides opportunities for planning a variety of buildings such as a tower, fort, castle, boat, rocket, landscape, mine or town. Damp sand is used and supplementary materials include pebbles, flags, dowels and toys such as lorries, bulldozers and rollers. This kind of building activity can be used to encourage the child to discuss and plan an activity before carrying it out. The child names the materials he will need and describes what he will do with them. The following example illustrates this procedure.

The child decides to build a tunnel. He first names the item he will use such as a spade, scoop, bulldozer and roller. He then describes his first step (e.g. 'I'm going to dig a hole in the side of the hill') before carrying it out. He continues to describe and then carry out the various stages until the tunnel is completed. He may of course encounter problems such as the tunnel collapsing. This provides the opportunity for him to discuss several solutions (e.g. using something to support the roof of the tunnel; adding a little more water to the sand and packing it more tightly; using a cardboard tube buried in sand; digging from opposite sides of the hill, and so on) before putting them to the test.

Problem-solving

Simple problems can be stated and several solutions discussed before testing them. For example, a problem such as:

How can you make a sandcastle collapse/fall?

might result in several answers such as:

Knock it down with a stick or spade
Dig away the sand at the bottom
Dig a hole (tunnel) under it
Drop something on it

which can be discussed before they are tried in practice.

Here are some examples of problems (several solutions for each can be discussed):

How do you make a tunnel?
How do you prevent a tall tower from collapsing?
How do you make a round, flat pancake?
How do you make a hill?
How do you draw a straight line in the sand?
How do you make a pattern of squares?
How do you make many small holes?

Twenty questions (A variation of this game is described in more detail on p. 64). The principle of this game involves asking questions to identify one object from a choice of several by including some possibilities and excluding others. The following example illustrates a procedure:

Two square flags and two triangular (pointed) flags are planted in the sand. One square flag and one pointed flag are green, the other two flags are red. A coin (treasure) is buried under one flag and the child need ask only two questions to identify the flag, for example:

Is it a square flag? (Yes)—this excludes both pointed flags.
Is it green? (No)—it must therefore be the square, red flag.

Home corner

The home corner should, if possible, be partitioned or screened from the rest of the classroom. Basic items of furniture such as a table, chairs, bed, cupboard and mirror should be kept to a minimum so that the area can readily be changed and adapted to fulfil a variety of functions ranging, for example, from a room to a setting or theme for a story.

Materials

Screen, divider, clothes-horse, curtains; table, chairs, bench, bed, storage boxes, bed-clothes; cooker, cupboard, shelves, pegs, clock, cookery set, cloth, mats; ingredients (e.g. flour, salt, sugar); saucepans, pots, crockery, cutlery, bowls; broom, brush, pan, bin; iron, ironing board; dolls, puppets.

Dressing-up materials: variety of long and short dresses, coats, cloaks, trousers; lengths of material, paper; uniforms—nurse, policeman, astronaut; caps, belts, helmets, crowns, badges, brooches, sashes, ribbons, spectacle frames, wigs, gloves, bags, walking stick, mirror.

Some examples of equipment and functions:

Kitchen—cooker, shelf, cooking utensils.

Living room—settee (adapted bed or bench), television set (box with transparent screen behind which pictures or puppets can be placed).

Hospital—extra beds (adapted benches or chairs), bedside tables (boxes).

Bus—seats and benches arranged in rows.

Fire engine—same as 'bus', with addition of ladder (chair) and hose (made of rope).

Dwelling—house, caravan, wigwam, igloo, hut.

'Stage' or setting—for stories such as 'Three little pigs', 'Goldilocks', 'The old woman who lived in a shoe'.

Dressing-up in appropriate clothes such as cook's apron, doctor's coat, fireman's helmet, driver's cap, etc., can help to stimulate role-playing and commentary.

Pictures and drawings with captions (these can also be incorporated in home-made books) relating to topics such as cooking, cleaning, hospital routine, journey/visit, story sequence, etc., can be used in conjunction with appropriate activities.

Topics and activities used to develop language skills:

Listening

Sounds in the home: cooking (frying, boiling), putting crockery and cutlery on the table, pouring tea, washing dishes; knocking on door, footsteps, hammering, sweeping, dusting, moving furniture, scrubbing; laughing, crying, snoring.

Naming, categorising, describing

Examples of categories and themes and respective individual items:

Family: mum, dad, brother, sister, baby

Furniture: chair, table, cupboard, shelf

People who help us: milkman, postman, doctor, painter, bus driver, dustman

Hospital: doctor, nurse, patient, medicine, ambulance.

Denoting position

Words denoting position such as on, next to, above, behind, corner, side and middle, can be encouraged in activities such as:

arranging furniture in a room

laying the table for tea

fighting a fire

arranging the stage or setting for a story.

Sequencing

Sequences can be used to focus on tenses and relational words of time such as first, before, after, when and while, in topics and activities such as:

Dressing-up—order in which clothes are put on/taken off

Hospital—general routine of arrival, treatment and discharge, daily routine of making beds, feeding and treating patients

Fire-fighting: alarm, mounting fire engine, fighting fire, rescue

Journey/Visit: preparing to leave, outward journey, place of interest, return home.

Reasoning

The topics and activities outlined above under sequencing can be used to encourage the child to plan and predict. Discussion—naming equipment needed, arranging the materials and planning the stages and sequences of events—is encouraged before actions are carried out.

Materials used in water play and building activities

Water play

Plastic bath (about 30 cm deep), water trough, large bucket, jug, scoop, sponge, cloth

Containers of various sizes: cups, mugs, liquid soap containers, bottles, buckets

Colander, tea strainer, funnels (wide, narrow), lengths of polythene tubing (wide, narrow), cylindrical container with holes punched at various heights

Collection of objects that float: cork, wood, toy boats, sponge

Collection of objects that sink: stone, spoon, shell, coin, cup filled with water, nail, button.

Variations to water obtained by adding: warm water, coloured powder, soap.

Building

Large apparatus—blocks, boards, interlocking blocks, boxes

Small apparatus—blocks (wood, plastic), cubes, pyramids, cylinders, wheels, dowel rods

Construction kits—interlocking blocks, playbricks, unifix blocks, magnetic bricks, Leggo, Tinkertoy, Meccano, interlocking plastic 'straws' with connecting pieces, pegboard with pegs and hooks, tracks, roadways, bridges

Tools and associated materials—hammer, saw, pliers, drill, screwdriver, nails, screws, nuts and bolts, planks, wood off-cuts, glue.

'Junk'—cardboard boxes, matchboxes, corrugated cardboard, cardboard cylinders, liquid soap containers, corks, cotton reels, boards, planks, wood off-cuts, shavings, pegboard, string, rope, rubber bands, glue.

Toys—vehicles, people, animals, tracks, fences, buildings, trees.

PART 3

Associated Activities and Resources

Chapter 9   Language games

Introduction

In order to concentrate on particular areas of language weakness, it is useful to devote a short period of the day (say, fifteen to twenty minutes at a regular time each morning) to special games and activities with particular children. For this short period the teacher can focus on one or two language skills, using a particular type of activity or game. The language games and other materials discussed in this section therefore are ancillary to the activities discussed in parts 1 and 2.

The games should not be used in isolation, but as part of an overall approach to helping language development. The rules and procedures outlined are intended as examples which can be adapted and extended by the teacher. Similarly the examples of illustrated picture cards can be copied or adapted to form the basis for a wider collection of materials. It is important that the child should become familiar with the pictures used and where possible have experience of the actual objects they represent. Some children may not easily see the relationship between objects and their pictorial representation.

Aims

The main aim of the language games is to give the child the opportunity to practise the language skills and patterns discussed in part 1 and to encourage purposeful verbal communication between children. The games can also be a means of helping the teacher to check on the child's progress in acquiring language.

Type of materials

(a) Large baseboards or squares of cardboard divided into smaller squares.
(b) Picture cards: usually pictures, drawings, or cards on which picture 'stamps' are pasted, (a wide variety of stamps is obtainable from educational equipment suppliers and publishers such as Philip & Tacey, Galt's, etc.).
(c) A selection of toys, counters, buttons, blocks, etc.

Type of games

Most of the rules and procedures outlined in this chapter are based on well-known games such as lotto and various card games which involve collecting, discarding and exchanging pictures. In playing the game the child makes various 'moves' and is encouraged to use appropriate language patterns. Before a game can be played satisfactorily, the children should be familiar with the procedure and language involved. Careful guidance and help from the teacher will be required in the early stages.

Instructions

Most of the instructions which follow can be used in conjunction with the picture cards suggested. The games include lotto (bingo), Kim's game, 'identikit', sorting and building. Each game is designed to give the child practice in specific language skills (identified in part 1). Each set of cards should be coded with an emblem to help sorting after use.

The games can be adapted and extended. Most of the games can be made more difficult by increasing the number of cards, and by introducing more complex pictures which require finer discriminations and more elaborate language patterns.

Listening and naming

Screen game

Aim. To give the child practice in recognising sounds and naming the objects and actions associated with them.

Materials. (a) Two sets of sound-producing materials such as a piece of paper, a bell, a small gong, a rubber band, a tumbler, sand, etc.

(b) A cardboard screen which is placed across the table between the children. (NB Screen can be simple cardboard pinned to table.)

Players. Two.

Procedure. Two players A and B are seated opposite each other on either side of the screen. Each player has a set of materials. Player A makes a sound (e.g. rings the bell), and B tries to produce a similar sound with his materials. (Because of the screen B cannot see A's materials, and he has to recognise the sound before choosing the appropriate materials.) B then makes a sound and A tries to match it. When the players become familiar with the game the player matching the sound also tries to name the apparatus and associated action.

Recognising and naming familiar sounds

Naming

Kim's game

Aim. To give the child practice in naming and remembering a number of pictures/objects.

   Materials. Picture cards—chair, shoe, dress, car, dog, coat, ice cream.

   Players. Two.

   Procedure. Any three cards are spread out on the table, face upwards. Player A names each card, then faces away while B turns one card over and rearranges the cards. (If objects are being used, one object can be hidden in a box or held under the table.) A then looks at the cards and tries to name the one which has been turned over. The procedure is repeated with A turning a card over and B trying to identify it.

   Variations. The cards can be changed, and as the players become familiar with the game the number of cards can be increased.

Kim's game

Naming and categorising

Animal lotto

Aim. To give the child practice in naming various animals and using basic sentence patterns.

Materials. (a) Four baseboards—each board contains four individual pictures (i.e. different combinations of animals such as dog, cat, elephant, cow, horse, etc.).

(b) A set of individual picture cards—one for each different animal on the baseboards.

(c) A set of sixteen counters or blank cards.

Players. Four (maximum) and one leader or 'caller'.

Procedure. Each player is given a baseboard and four counters. The leader or caller has the set of five individual picture cards. The players are told that they are going to play animal lotto, and they are to look at the picture card and name the animal. They take it in turns to answer. (It is useful to keep to a definite order when taking turns: for example, clockwise, starting with the first player on the leader's left.)

The leader holds up the first card from his pack, so that all the players can see it, and asks, 'What is this (picture)?'

The player whose turn it is says, for example, 'It's a cat.'

When the card has been correctly named, the leader then asks each player in turn if he has a cat. Each player should be encouraged to answer in a complete sentence such as, 'I've got a cat', before placing a counter on the appropriate picture on his board. The player who has not got the picture replies appropriately, for example, 'I haven't got a cat'. The game continues until all the pictures on each board are covered. The players can then change boards and the game is repeated. The players can also take turns at being the leader.

Variations (a) To avoid unnecessary repetition a greater variety of picture cards can be used so that no more than, say, two players have pictures of the same animal.

(b) If enough dealer's cards are available the players can 'win' a card from the dealer instead of covering up a picture on their baseboard with a blank card.

Note. These instructions can also be used with picture-cards belonging to categories such as:

People/family (man, woman, boy, girl, baby, mum, dad, etc.)

Clothes (coat, shoes, dress, trousers, hat, etc.)

Furniture (chair, table, cupboard, bed, etc.)

Food (apple, banana, carrot, potato, bread, etc.)

Food can be sub-divided into fruit, vegetables, etc.

Vehicle transport (car, lorry, bus, bicycle, etc.)

Music/musical instruments (piano, recorder, triangle, drum, etc.)

The baseboard and individual cards for Animal lotto

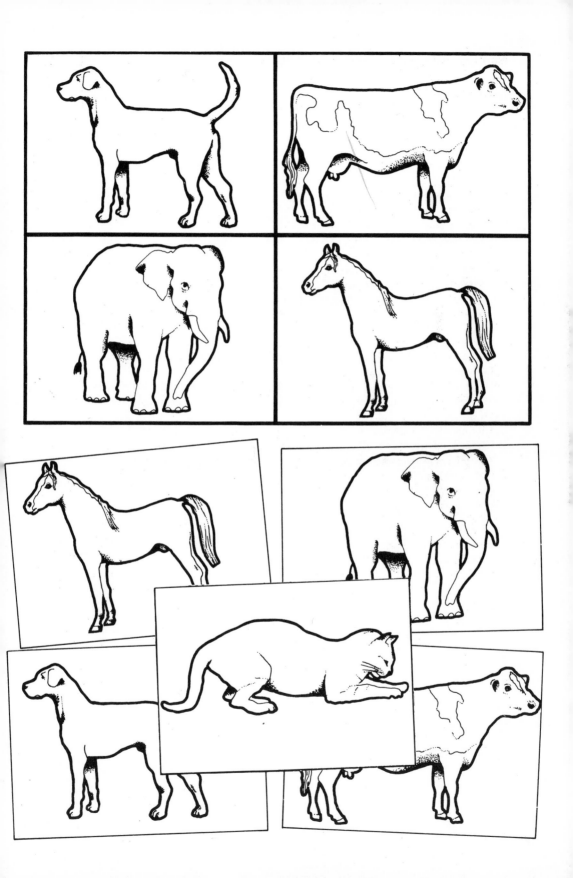

Naming, categorising and describing

Linking pictures

Aim. To give the child practice in naming or describing pictures and associating pairs of pictures.

Materials. (a) A baseboard containing two columns of squares approximately four inches apart (see illustration).

(b) Pairs of picture cards such as brush/pan, iron/ironing board, boot/football, saucepan/stove, and so on.

(c) About eight lengths of string or narrow cardboard strips, about 30 cm in length and each a different colour.

Players. Two.

Procedure. The picture cards can be placed in any order on the squares on the baseboard providing that one member of each pair is in a different column to its 'partner'. Thus the brush might be in the top square of the left-hand column and the pan might be in the third-from-top square of the right-hand column, and so on. The first child takes a piece of string and places one end on a picture in the left-hand column and the other on the associated picture in the right-hand column. He makes short statements about the pictures he has linked.

Example: The brush goes with the pan . . . We sweep dust into the pan with the brush.

The second player does likewise, using another piece of string to link two more pictures while making an appropriate statement.

Variations. The game can be made more difficult by increasing the number of pictures in the columns, and by using pairs of pictures which are less obviously associated with each other.

The following examples of pairs are based on categories (sorting activities):

hat/sock (clothes), apple/banana (fruit), hammer/pliers (tools), car/train (transport).

The following examples of picture pairs are linked because of similarities in sounds (initial sounds and vowel sounds) or visual spelling patterns:

chair/chain, thorn/thumb, shoe/sheep, etc.

dog/log, bin/pin, tail/nail, etc.

Cards arranged on a baseboard in columns

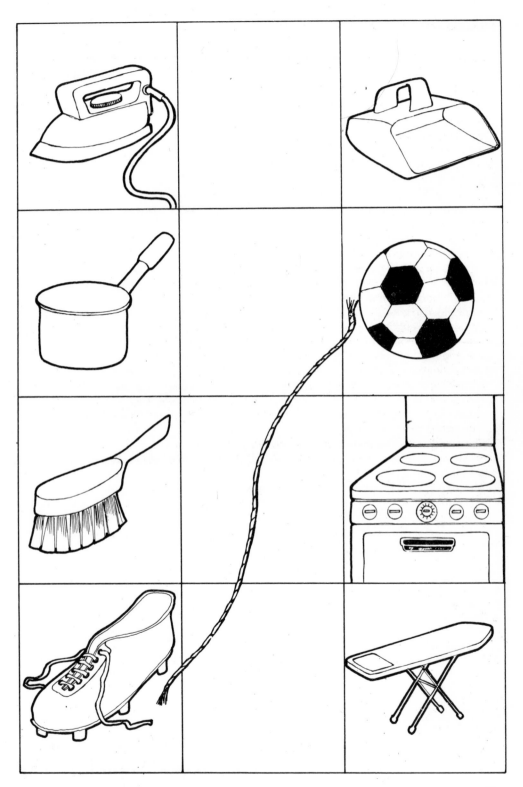

Describing

'What is he/she wearing?' lotto

Aim. To give the child practice in naming and describing (colour and size) the clothes worn by a number of men or women.

Materials. (a) Four baseboards—each board contains four individual pictures, i.e. different combinations of men's clothes such as:

hat, long red coat, white trousers
no hat, long red coat, white trousers
no hat, short blue coat, black trousers
hat, long blue coat, white trousers
no hat, short red coat, black trousers.

(b) A set of individual picture cards which represent each different combination of clothes in (a) above.

(c) A set of sixteen counters or blank cards.

Players. Four (maximum), and one leader.

Procedure. Each player is given a baseboard and four counters. The leader has the set of individual picture cards. The players are told that they are going to play 'What is he wearing?' lotto, and that they are to look at the picture and describe (talk about) the clothes the man is wearing. They take it in turns to answer. (It is useful to keep to a definite order when taking turns: for example, clockwise, starting with the first player on the leader's left.) The leader holds up the first card from his pack, so that all the players can see it, and asks, 'What is this man wearing?' The player whose turn it is says, for example, 'He's wearing a hat and a long blue coat and white trousers'.

When the clothes have been correctly described, the leader asks each player in turn if he has a man 'with a hat, long blue coat and white trousers'. Each player should be encouraged to give a full description of the clothes before placing a counter on the appropriate picture on his board.

The game continues until all the pictures on each board are covered. The players can then change boards and the game is repeated. The players can also take turns at being the leader.

Variation. To avoid unnecessary repetition a greater variety of picture cards can be used so that no more than, say, two players have the same picture of a combination of clothes.

A baseboard and individual cards showing some of the possible combinations (tints indicate different colours)

'Identikit'—clothes

Aim. To give the child practice in naming and describing (colour and size) the clothes worn by a number of men/women.

Materials. (a) Four 'complete' pictures of men dressed in clothes of the following combinations:

hat, long blue coat, white trousers
hat, short blue coat, black trousers
no hat, long red coat, white trousers
no hat, short red coat, black trousers.

(b) A similar set of the above pictures each cut horizontally into three so that there are twelve strips of card with the following parts which can be combined to make complete pictures:

two heads with hats
two heads without hats
one long red coat
one short red coat
one long blue coat
one short blue coat
two pairs white trousers
two pairs black trousers.

Players. Two.

Procedure. Two players A and B are seated opposite each other at a table. A has set (a), and B has set (b). The players are told that A will describe what the man is wearing and B will try to put the strips together to make his man look the same. The players can ask and answer questions, but they are not allowed to point.

B first sorts the four heads (in any order) in a horizontal line, then the four coats (in any order) in a horizontal line under the heads, and then the four pairs of trousers.

Player A places his cards in a pack face downward on the table, picks up the first one and holds it so that B cannot see the picture (if necessary, a screen can be placed between the players). A then describes the clothes starting with the head, then the jacket and then the trousers.

Example of description: 'He is wearing a hat, a blue coat—a long blue coat and white trousers.'

After B has assembled his picture, both players check to see if it is the same as A's picture. The procedure is repeated until all four pictures have been assembled. The players then exchange their sets of cards so that B instructs and A assembles.

Variations. The combinations of clothes can be varied, and new clothes and colours can be introduced.

The sample pictures. The dotted lines indicate where the complete picture must be cut to produce the horizontal strips (tints indicate different colours)

'Identikit'—face

Aim. To give the child practice in naming and describing parts of the face.

Materials. (a) Three complete pictures of a face:

Black hair, no glasses, no beard

Fair (yellow) hair, blue glasses, no beard

Black hair, no glasses, black beard.

(b) A similar set of the above pictures, each cut horizontally into three so that there are nine strips of card with the following parts which can be combined to make complete faces:

one fair hair

two black hair

one pair yellow glasses

one pair blue glasses

one pair eyes without glasses

one fair beard

one black beard

one chin without beard.

Players. Two.

Procedure. Two players A and B are seated opposite each other at a table. A has set (a) and B has set (b). The players are told that A will describe a picture of a face and B will try to put the strips together to make a face which looks the same as A's picture. The players can ask and answer questions but they are not allowed to point.

B first sorts the three sets of hair (in any order) in a horizontal line, then the four pairs of eyes and glasses in a line under the sets of hair, and then the chins. Player A places his cards in a pack face downward on the table, picks up the first one and holds it so that B cannot see the picture (if necessary a screen can be placed between the players). A then describes the face while B tries to assemble a similar face.

Example of description: Black hair, blue glasses . . . he has no beard.

After B has assembled the face both players check to see if it is the same as A's picture. The procedure is then repeated until all three faces have been assembled. The players then exchange their sets of cards, and reverse roles.

Variations. Differences in features can be introduced, e.g. colour of eyes, length and shape of nose, size of ears, etc.

Two sample pictures. The dotted lines indicate where the complete picture must be cut to produce the horizontal strips (tints indicate different colours)

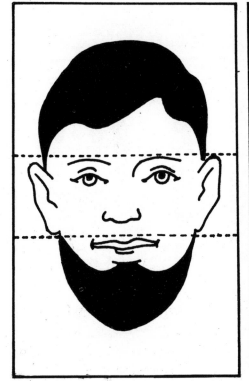

Categorising

Sorting (using sorting trays)

Aim. To give the child practice in naming pictures (of individual items) and sorting them into various categories.

Materials. (a) Category cards—clothes, animals, furniture, tools.

(b) Individual cards—dress, tie, coat (jacket), shoes; dog, horse, elephant, cat; table, chair, cupboard, bed; hammer, pliers, drill, saw.

(c) Four shallow sorting boxes (large enough to contain a category card).

Players. Four.

Procedure. A category card is placed in each of the four sorting boxes. The sixteen individual cards are placed in a pack face downward on the table between the four players.

Each player takes one sorting box and names the group or category (e.g. clothes) he is collecting. Each player then takes it in turns (in a clockwise direction) to pick up a card, name it and say whether it belongs to his group or not. If the card does not belong, he places it face downward at the bottom of the pack.

The game continues until each player has collected all the cards in his category. The individual cards are then collected and shuffled, the players exchange sorting boxes and the game starts again.

A sample category card and individual cards

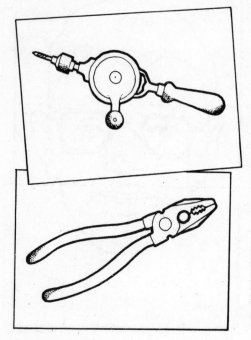
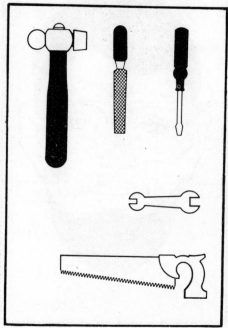

Naming and categorising

Sorting (using baseboards)

Aim. To give the child practice in naming pictures (of individual items) and sorting them into categories. The following categories are included in this game:

    animals, clothes, food, tools, people, furniture, vehicles, weapons.

    Materials. (a) A set of sixteen pictures, each consisting of an example of one of the eight categories. (There are two examples per category—dog and elephant for animal; ice-cream and cake for food, etc.)

    (b) Two baseboards. Each baseboard is made up of four pictures of the categories mentioned above (animals, clothes, etc.)

    Players. Two, seated opposite each other.

    Procedure. Each player is given a baseboard. The sixteen pictures are shuffled and placed in a pack, face downward, between the two players.

    Each player, in turn, picks up a card from the pack. He names the card, and if it belongs to one of the categories on his board, he names the category it belongs to and places the picture on the appropriate place on his board.

    Example of a sentence pattern which might be used: 'This is a dog. I put it with these animals'.

    If the card does not belong to one of his categories he returns it, face downward, to the bottom of the pack. Each player tries to collect two pictures (or four or five, as the child becomes more familiar with the game) for each category. When each board is completed the cards are collected, shuffled and placed face downward between the players, who then exchange boards and proceed to take turns in picking up cards from the pack.

    Variation. The game can be made more difficult by increasing the number of categories and the number of items belonging to each category.

A sample baseboard and individual cards

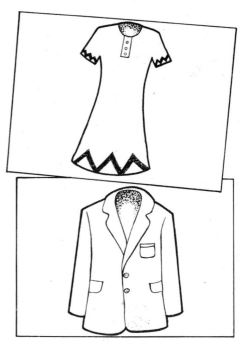

Describing and denoting position

Building game
Aim. To give the child practice in naming and describing objects (such as red block, green car and cork), and denoting the position of an object in relation to other objects.
Materials.
(a) A set of the following pictures (or models):
Tower—blocks, cork
Tower—block, cotton reels
Tower—large and small blocks
Train—blocks, cork
Bridge—blocks, cardboard, car, cork
Bridge/crane—blocks, pencil, car, string
Ramp—blocks, cardboard strip
House—blocks, cardboard.
(b) the following items:
Toy cars and lorries
Blocks of various colours
Corks, cotton reels, strips of cardboard, piece of string (with loops at either end).
Players. Two.
Procedure. Two players A and B are seated opposite each other. A has the set of pictures arranged in a pack and placed face downward in front of him, and B has the materials. The players are told that A will tell B how to make a 'building'. They can ask and answer questions but they must not point.

B moves all his toys to one side (they can be placed in an open box or tray), leaving a clear area in front of him. A picks up the first card and holds it so that B cannot see the picture. (A cardboard screen can be placed between the two players so they cannot see each other's picture or materials.) A then gives instructions such as: 'Take the yellow block and the green block . . . put the green block on the yellow block . . . put the cork on the green block'.

After B has assembled the tower, both players check to see if the model is the same as A's picture. The players can then change places and repeat the procedure—this time B instructs and A builds. The procedure is repeated using the next card and so on.

Building cards for making a tower, bridge, train and house using blocks, corks, cotton reels and cardboard

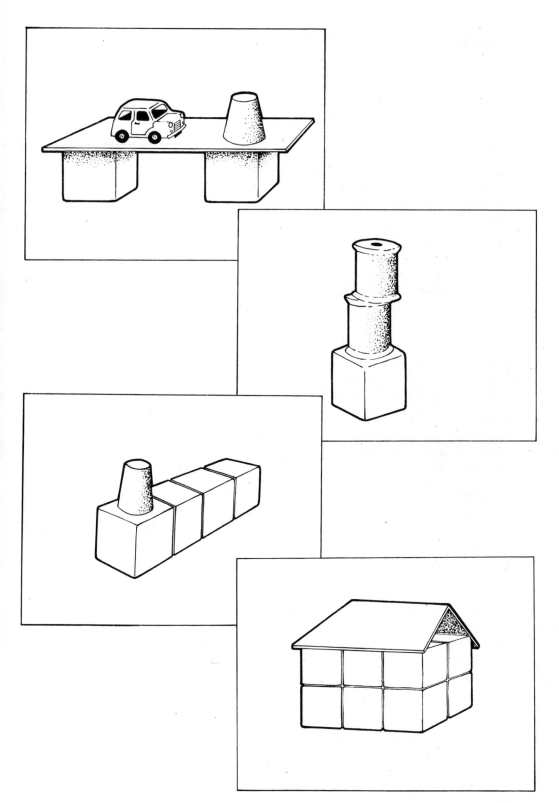

Denoting position

'Where's the cup?' lotto

Aim. To give the child practice in using appropriate words to denote an object's position in relation to its surroundings: e.g. 'in the box', 'behind the box', 'between the boxes', etc.

Materials. (a) Four baseboards. Each board contains four individual pictures, i.e. various pictures showing a cup in different positions in relation to other objects in the picture: in the box, behind the box, between the boxes, etc.

(b) Individual cards which represent each different card on the baseboards.

(c) A set of sixteen counters or blank cards.

Players. Four (maximum) and one leader.

Procedure. Each player is given a baseboard and four counters. The leader has the set of individual cards.

The players are told that they are going to play 'Where's the cup?' lotto, and they are to look at the pictures and say where the cup is. They take it in turns to answer. (It is useful to keep to a definite order when taking turns: for example, clockwise, starting with the first player on the leader's left.)

The leader holds up the first card from his pack, so that all the players can see it, and asks, 'Where is the cup?'

The player whose turn it is says, for example: 'The cup is in the box'.

When the position of the cup has been correctly denoted, the leader then asks each player in turn if he has a card with the cup in the box. Each player should be encouraged to answer in a complete sentence, such as 'I've got a cup in the box', before placing a counter on the appropriate picture on his board.

The game continues until all the pictures on each board are covered. The players can then change boards and the game is repeated. The players can also take turns in being the leader.

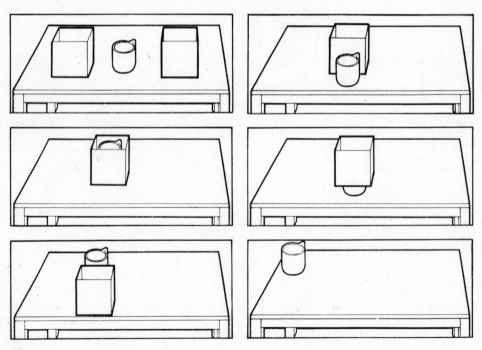

Naming and describing

Match a colour, win a picture

Aim. To give the child practice in matching colours and naming or describing pictures.

Materials. (a) A baseboard which is divided into six squares. Each square is a different colour.

(a) A set of picture cards similar to those used in various lotto games (described on p. 46).

(c) A box containing six strips of coloured paper. Each strip of paper matches a different coloured square on the master board.

Players. Two, three or four.

Procedure. A different picture card is placed on each coloured square on the base-board. The remaining cards are placed in a pack near the board. The first player draws a coloured strip of paper from the box. If he can name or describe the picture on the square which matches his strip of paper, he 'wins' the picture. This picture is then replaced on the board by another picture from the pack, and the coloured strip is returned to the box which is shaken before the next player takes his turn.

Variations. (a) The set of picture cards can be changed so that different language skills are emphasized. Cards can range in complexity from single objects, requiring simple language patterns for naming, to more detailed pictures requiring descriptions of colour, size, position etc. (See p. 47 for illustrations of cards.)

(b) The squares on the board can be numbered (in rows from left to right), and a die can be used to indicate the numbered square from which to 'win' the picture.

Individual cards showing the cup in different positions

Sequencing

Tell the story

Aim. To give the child practice in arranging pictures in sequence, and narrating the events depicted, using relational words of time such as 'then', 'before' and 'after', and appropriate tenses.

Materials. A number of large theme cards such as cooking, mending and painting. For each theme card there is a set of three smaller sequence cards. For example, cooking has a theme card on which are depicted all the main items in the sequence, e.g. the cook, bowl, spoon, ingredients and cooker. Each of the three sequence cards for cooking depicts an event: the first is pouring the ingredients into the bowl, the second is stirring the mixture, and the third is putting the cake in the oven. (See illustration opposite for examples of theme and sequence cards.)

Players. Two to four.

Procedure. The teacher discusses each theme card in turn, encouraging the children to name the main items (e.g. cook, bowl, spoon, etc.) on the card. The teacher then discusses the sequence of events using the sequence cards and focusing on words such as 'before', 'after', 'while', etc. Each player is then given one theme card. All the smaller cards (twelve cards, if there are four players) are shuffled and placed in a pack, face downward, in the centre of the table. Each player takes it in turn (in a clockwise direction) to pick up a card, retain it if it belongs to his theme card or return it, face downward, to the bottom of the pack.

If he retains the card, he describes what is happening, for example: 'She is mixing (stirring) with a spoon'.

When the players have each collected the three cards belonging to their set (theme), they arrange them in sequence (from left to right). Each player is then encouraged to 'tell the story' about the cards. The players can then exchange theme cards and the smaller cards are collected and shuffled and the same procedure is repeated.

Variations. After each player has had a chance to 'tell the story', they are asked to look at their set of cards and find the card which the teacher describes. If they can identify it correctly, they place it in the centre of the table. In describing the cards the teacher uses relational words of time, such as before and after, to distinguish one card from another. For example, in the cooking sequence the questions might be:

Which picture shows what the cook does before she mixes the cake?

Which picture shows what the cook does after she mixes the cake?

Which picture shows what the cook does before she puts the cake in the oven? (there are two correct choices here).

A sample theme card on cooking and three smaller sequence cards

Reasoning

Twenty questions

Aim. To help the child to ask questions to identify a picture, from a choice of several pictures, by including some possibilities and excluding others.

Materials. Four cards:

(a) man in blue coat
(b) man in red coat
(c) woman in blue coat
(d) woman in red coat

A small coin (or any small flat object which can be hidden under a card).

Players. One child and teacher.

Procedure. Cards (a) and (b) are placed in front of the child. A small coin is hidden under one of the cards while the child looks away. The teacher then encourages him to ask questions in order to find out which card is covering the coin. The child must not point. (Instead of hiding a coin under one card, the teacher can simply ask 'Which picture am I thinking about?') Several demonstrations may be necessary in order to convey to the child the idea of the game. If, for example, the child asks, 'Is it the man in the blue coat?' and the answer is 'No', then it must be the other card. (The use of negative information in this way is an important principle of the game.) The procedure is repeated using cards (c) and (d), and then using any two cards several times, varying the card which covers the coin.

When the child has got used to the idea of the game, all four cards can be used. The child is encouraged to identify the card by asking only two questions. For example:

Is it a man?   (No)
Is she wearing red?   (No)
It's the woman in blue.

It is helpful in the early stages to cover up (or move to one side) those cards which are eliminated. In the example above, when the child learns that it is not a man, he moves the two men to one side and his next question relates to the colour of the women's clothes.

Suggestions for other materials:

Dolls: boy in blue, boy in red, girl in blue, girl in red
Blocks: big yellow, big green, small yellow, small green
Animals: big cat, big dog, small cat, small dog
Vehicles: black car, red car, black lorry, red lorry
Flags planted in sand tray: square yellow, 'pointed' (triangular) yellow, square green, pointed green ('treasure' is buried under one of the flags)
Children: boy and girl wearing hats, boy and girl without hats.

Sample cards showing possible combinations (tints indicate different colours)

64

Picture reading

Aim. To encourage the child to make a number of verbal guesses (relating to a picture) based on a limited amount of information (only part of the picture can be seen). It is not intended that the child's guesses should be 'correct', but that there should be a reasoned discussion based on limited clues.

Materials. (a) Any large, clear picture of a familiar scene or activity can be used. A picture of an accident scene is used in this game as an example.

(b) A larger sheet of card with a hole approximately half an inch square cut in the centre is used to cover the picture.

Players. One to four.

Procedure. The picture is covered with the sheet of card so that only a car can be seen. The children are asked to guess what else might be in the picture. They are encouraged to use language patterns which incorporate words such as: might, could be, if, but, or.

Example of language patterns: 'I think it's a car . . . it could be going along the road . . . there might also be a bus and a lorry in the picture. The car has had a crash . . . it might have hit another car or a wall,' etc.

When the children have discussed a variety of possibilities, the teacher moves the covering card revealing another part of the picture. The children continue to discuss various possibilities, ruling out some of the previous suggestions as a result of what is now revealed. The covering card can be moved several times (discussion is encouraged after each move) before it is taken away so that the whole picture can be seen. A new picture is then covered and the whole procedure is repeated.

Picture card of a road accident and accompanying blank card with a square hole in the centre

Chapter 10   The tape recorder and recorded materials

Introduction

This chapter does not give a comprehensive coverage of the wide range of uses to which the cassette recorder can be put. Instead we provide some introductory notes and three examples of programmes which are intended to indicate possible uses of the cassette recorder and to suggest ways in which teachers can make their own materials.

Cassette recorders: some practical considerations

The cassette recorder can be used to supplement the work of the teacher by giving children the opportunity to hear stories repeated and to practise following instructions. An important advantage of recorded material is that it provides a form of individual and personal communication. Most children readily accept the recorded voice, and soon become accustomed to carrying out instructions and answering questions, providing that the programmes are based on situations with which they are familiar.

A major drawback in using a conventional 'spool to spool' tape recorder in the classroom is that it usually requires frequent supervision by the teacher: there are problems of operating controls and finding the place on the tape in order to select the programme or hear sections repeated. These problems have been overcome to some extent by the cassette recorder/playback type of machine (with piano key controls) which can be operated by young children.

The Synchrofax audio page

The Synchrofax is a recording/playback machine. It is a box which can be situated conveniently on a desk top or table.

The worksheets are designed to present visual and auditory material simultaneously. Pictures, diagrams or words can be drawn or glued on the upper surface. The under surface contains magnetic material for recording instructions or information relating to the visual display.

When in use the worksheet is placed on top of the Synchrofax, and covered by a transparent top. The recorded material can be played while the worksheet is in position. A set of piano-key controls enables the pupil to switch the machine on or off and to rewind or wind forward.

Worksheets are obtainable in blank form. There is also a range of commercially produced pre-recorded materials in the fields of reading (including 'phonics'), basic number work and elementary science.

Further details are obtainable from: E. J. Arnold Ltd, Butterley Street, Leeds LS10 1AX.

The Language Master (Bell & Howell A-V Ltd.)

This machine is used in conjunction with rectangular strips of card which contain magnetic recording tape. The card is fed into a channel at the top of the machine (this can easily be done by young children) and a recording is automatically played back as the card moves through the channel. About eight seconds of recording time are provided (this amount can be reduced by cutting the card into smaller pieces). The machine also has the facility for allowing the child to respond to the recorded instructions by passing the same card through the machine while turning the appropriate knob and recording his own voice.

The Language Master is ideally suited for recording short instructions such as:

Fill the red bucket with sand.

Colour the man's coat blue.

Put all the animals in the field.

or for recording a series of instructions which can be divided into short sections. The Language Master cards can be arranged in the appropriate order and stacked in an open box or tray. The child can follow the instructions step by step, at his own pace (repeating sections if necessary). Here is an example of part of a series of instructions:

card 1   Put two chairs near the table.

card 2   Put two plates on the table.

card 3   Put a spoon next to each plate, etc.

Preparing and recording programmes

The making of recorded material usually involves at least three stages: writing the script, e.g. stories and instructions based on activities carried out in the classroom; trying out the script by reading it while a child follows the directions (this helps the teacher to gauge the pace and timing of the reading); recording the script and, where appropriate, 'mixing' in sound effects such as splashing water, knocking and opening door, footsteps, etc.

Although individual teachers can record their own materials, there are obvious advantages in establishing small groups of teachers for producing master tapes for multi-copying. Ideas can be exchanged and scripts written, while the facilities in a teachers' centre or resources centre can be used for recording, mixing sounds and editing. Copies made from master tapes can be distributed to schools.

Suggestions for programmes

Stories

There are many commercially produced stories, verses and songs available on disc and cassette. Stories recorded by the teacher can be used in conjunction with an illustrated book. The child turns the pages while the story is being narrated; he is given cues (usually the sound of a chime or bell) at appropriate points in the story. A slide projector can be used instead of a book; an advantage of using coloured slides is that the pictures projected can be seen by a large group of children.

There are advantages in giving the child the opportunity to listen to familiar stories without the support of illustrations. In doing so the child has to listen attentively to the language in order to follow the story. Occasional sound-effects (dog barking, water splashing, etc.) where relevant, can help to stimulate the child's imagination and maintain his interest.

Instructions

There are many different kinds of tasks which the child can carry out by following recorded instructions. Some examples of activities include building, moving objects, playing a game (e.g. lotto) and colouring-in. Large cards with drawings of houses, trees and fences, or shapes such as circles, squares and stars can be used in conjunction with familiar objects such as buttons, blocks, coins, pencils, string, various toys, etc., to give the child practice in following instructions. The following extracts, focusing on describing (shape and colour), and denoting position suggest the type of script which could be extended and adapted for recording:

Using card illustration . . . Put the white button on the red house . . . the cork between the green tree and the fence . . . the car next to the . . . and so on. The child can then be asked where various objects are.

Examples:

Where is the white button? . . . Yes it's on the red house.

Which is nearer the green tree—the car or the cork? . . . Yes, the cork is nearer the green tree.

Using card illustration . . . Put the red pencil on the card so that one end of the pencil is on the square and the other end is on the star . . . now put the brown pencil so that one end is on the star and the . . . and so on. The child continues to 'join up' the shapes, making a triangular border or 'fence' around a 'paddock'. He or she then proceeds to sort a number of toy animals, putting some inside and some outside the 'paddock'.

Sample card showing a house, trees and fence

Sample card showing a circle, square and star

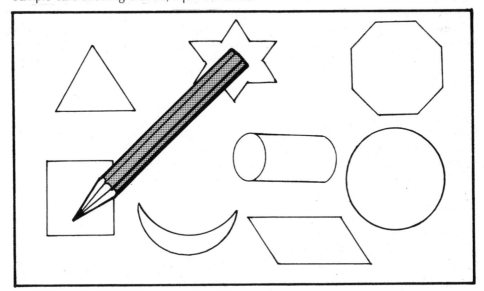

Recordings

The following scripts, which may be recorded by the teacher, are examples of programmes designed to give the child practice in listening to stories and carrying out instructions. The language skills given particular emphasis include: listening (sounds), naming, describing (colour) and denoting position.

Script 1 is a short story with sound effects. No ancillary materials are required.

Script 2 is a type of 'sound lotto'. The child is required to recognize four different sounds and place coloured cards over the picture which correspond with the sounds. Ancillary materials for this game are:

Four picture cards—baby, hammer, dog, car, (supplied with the tape)

Four colour cards—blue, red, yellow, green, (not supplied).

Script 3 is a building game. The child is required to build a tower and then a bridge using the following materials:

red block, yellow block (these should be fairly large), cotton reel,

strip of cardboard, toy car, (materials not supplied).

Script 1

This is a story about a boy called Mike and a dog called Spot. They were very good friends, and Spot liked to follow Mike wherever he went. One day when they were walking to the shops, Spot saw another dog on the other side of the road. He started to bark (bark) and then tried to run across the road.

'Look out!' shouted Mike. 'There's a car coming!'

The car hooted (horn) and Spot just managed to jump out of the way.

'Come here, you naughty dog,' said Mike. 'It's too dangerous playing near the street, let's go to the park instead.'

Spot liked playing in the park. He ran across the grass and jumped over the hedges. Suddenly he stopped. There was a cat hiding behind some bushes. 'Miaow (miaow)' said the cat.

Spot growled (growl) and before Mike could stop him Spot raced after the cat as fast as he could go. But the cat was too quick for Spot, and it climbed to the top of a tall tree, where Spot could not reach it.

'Come on let's go home' said Mike. But Spot didn't listen. He was standing by a pond looking at the goldfish swimming in the water. He leaned forward over the edge trying to catch a fish, and suddenly he overbalanced and fell into the water (splash).

Mike pulled Spot out of the water and they walked slowly home. Spot was feeling very wet, cold and sad. He would not run away from Mike again.

Script 2

We are going to play a game called 'sounds and pictures'. When you hear a sound like this (dog barking) try to find the picture of something that makes that sound. Listen to the sound again (dog barking). Put the red card on the picture that goes with that sound (pause). Now listen to this sound (car engine). Put the green card on the picture that goes with this sound (pause).

Now listen to the third sound (baby crying). Put the yellow card on the picture that goes with this sound.

Here's another sound (hammering). Put the blue card on the picture that goes with this sound (pause).

Now see if you can name the pictures. First pick up the red card and name the picture that the red card was covering (pause). It's the dog. Now pick up the green card. Which picture was the green card covering? (pause). It's the car.

Now pick up the yellow card. Which picture was the yellow card covering? (pause). It's the baby.

Now pick up the blue card. Which picture was the blue card covering? (pause). It's the hammer.

You have finished the game now, so put all the coloured cards together on the table. That's the end of the game called 'sounds and pictures'.

Script 3
We are going to play the 'building game'. Look at the toys on the table. Can you see the big red block and the big yellow block? There is also a cotton reel, a long piece of cardboard and a car.

I am going to tell you how to make a tower. Put the red block on top of the yellow block (pause). Look at the yellow block—can you see it is under the red block? Now put the cotton reel on top of the red block (pause). There, you have made a tower with a yellow block at the bottom, a red block in the middle and a cotton reel at the top. Now I want you to make a bridge. Put the cotton reel and the red block on the table near the yellow block (pause). Now move the cotton reel between the red block and the yellow block (pause). Look at the blocks and the cotton reel—the cotton reel is in the middle, the yellow block is on one side of the cotton reel, and the red block is on the other side of the cotton reel.

Put the long piece of cardboard on the red block and the yellow block—the cardboard is on both blocks (pause). You have made a bridge with cardboard and two blocks. The cotton reel is under the bridge. Put the car on the bridge (pause).

You have finished now, so put the car and the cardboard on the table next to the blocks. That's the end of the 'building game'.

A note on resources
Cassette recorders
There is a wide range of conventional tape and cassette recorders from which to choose and it is suggested that advice is sought locally before purchasing.

Here is a selection of addresses from which specifications and information on tapes, cassettes, discs and slides may be obtained: Educational Foundation for Visual Aids, 33 Queen Anne Street, London W1. Information and advice regarding virtually all aspects of audio and visual materials may also be obtained from: The School Broadcasting Council, B.B.C., The Langham, Portland Place, London W1A 1AA (also B.B.C. Radio Enterprises at the same address).

General information regarding school broadcasts can be obtained from the B.B.C. whose catalogue *Radio and television for children of 5–13* contains details of programmes and available materials.

Radio programmes for infants include:

Poetry corner (poems, rhymes and music); Let's join in (stories);

Music and movement (mime, rhythm, etc.).

Advice on taping programmes 'off the air' and the use of 'radio vision' (recorded material used in conjunction with slides) is available from: Weston Woods Studios Ltd., P.O. Box 2, Henley on Thames.

Catalogue containing annotated lists of slides and film strips based on well known children's stories and lists of recordings on cassette of stories and songs are available from: E. J. Arnold, Butterley Street, Leeds LS10 1AX.

This company also produces recorded programmes such as 'sound lotto', 'pictures in sound' and various instruction games.

Chapter 11   Reading activities

Reading should not be regarded as a separate topic which is dealt with in isolation, but as something closely associated with many of the activities in and outside the classroom. This chapter is not intended to provide a comprehensive reading programme, but to offer a number of suggestions with examples of activities and games which can help the child to understand something about the reading process and its relevance to his interests. An important underlying aim is to develop and maintain the child's motivation to learn to read.

Many children are strongly motivated to learn to read. Through observing and listening to parents reading newspapers, magazines and books, and through asking questions relating to these activities, the child gradually develops a general idea that reading is a process of communication: that the marks (print) on paper are a means of receiving information or 'finding out', that there is some equivalence between the symbols on paper and the language he hears and speaks. Frequent demands such as: 'Read this to me', 'What does this say?' and 'What word is this?' indicate an increasing awareness and understanding of some important concepts underlying reading, and of course a keen desire to learn to read. Other children, lacking this kind of contact with reading material and the opportunity to talk about reading, are unlikely to have the same enthusiasm and motivation. Further problems arise from the lack of understanding of important concepts such as: reading, telling a story, writing, drawing, and sound, word, sentence, etc. which are often used in talking about reading and in reading instruction.

We now look at three broad approaches which can be used as an introduction to the teaching of reading. These approaches, 'reading in everyday situations', 'reading games' and 'reading activities in the classroom', are discussed separately, but should be regarded as overlapping activities which are closely related to the general activities of the school.

Reading in everyday situations
There are many opportunities for drawing the child's attention to written language in familiar situations. The following common examples can be used to discuss the purpose and relevance of written words:

street names, signposts
indicator panel on a bus, on which is written the names of streets (indicating its route)
name tags on clothes; also name tags in school cloakroom, labels on boxes, bottles and other articles in shops
makes of cars; advertisements in shops, on display boards, on television; captions relating to pictures, book covers, print in story books, newspapers.

Reading games
Find the hidden object. This kind of game is intended to convey the principle that messages can be communicated via symbols. A child in a group or class is asked to hide an object, say a toy car, anywhere in the room so that no one coming into the room will know where it is. When the object is hidden the teacher writes on a blackboard or large sheet of paper, so that the children can see: 'The car is hidden behind the cupboard.'

An older child from another classroom is invited into the room and asked to find the hidden object. The teacher indicates the writing on the board which the older child reads, and then of course, finds the car behind the cupboard. This procedure can be repeated and varied so that a number of 'secrets' known only to the members of the group are 'decoded' by older children coming into the room and looking at the 'marks' on the board made by the teacher. It can also be shown that, by erasing one or two words from the message, the child who is reading the words can find out only part of the information: the name of the object, but not its whereabouts; the hiding place, but not the name of the object; and so on. In discussing the various activities involved in this game, the teacher can focus on important concepts such as 'reading', 'words', etc.

Symbols. A group of children can be encouraged to make up their own coding system for conveying messages to members of the group. The children should realize that any symbols can be devised providing that all the members of the group know what the symbols represent before they can communicate with each other. Some of the symbols can be made to resemble the word they represent: a pin-man drawing for 'man', a pair of legs for 'walking', a square for 'box', and so on. These can be supplemented by symbols such as straight lines, curved lines, arrows and circles which represent other words such as 'the', 'a', 'on', 'is', etc.

A small number of words can be used initially. For example, symbols for the words car, box, the, is, on, under can be drawn on separate cards, and the children arrange the symbols in various combinations to produce phrases and sentences such as:

the car and the box
The car is on the box.
The box is on the car.
The car is under the box.

Children can take turns in arranging and reading these symbols: one child gives instructions via the symbols, while another moves the box and car accordingly. Children are encouraged to make as many combinations as possible (including 'nonsense' sentences). At a later stage this kind of game can form the basis of discussions about the symbols for words in conventional writing.

Oral/auditory language games. Games such as 'I spy', which draw attention to the sounds of words, can help the child become aware of the component sounds of words. The leader pronounces the first sound (or sounds) e.g. 'b' of a familiar word. The other children try to identify the word by naming block, ball, boy, etc., until they guess correctly. Similarly, rhyming words can be used: a starter such as 'hat' can lead to guesses such as cat, mat, rat, etc.

Another type of game which draws attention to the component sounds of words is to present several pairs of pictures which have similar sounding names. The teacher (or leader) names one of the pictures and the child tries to identify it. Examples of similar sounding pairs and groups of words include: pig/peg, log/leg, dog/dig, foot/feet, car/cart/cat.

In order to help the child become aware of certain patterns (word order) in his language, the teacher can make up a short nonsense sentence, saying, for example, 'dog cat the chasing the is', and the child attempts to 'rearrange' these words (orally) in an acceptable pattern. This game can be adapted at a later stage so that word labels or flash cards are presented in scrambled form and the child tries to arrange them (visually) in an acceptable order.

Reading activities in the classroom

We stress that the examples below are intended as illustrations of the use of cards on which words are written, and include words and phrases which may be difficult: the teacher can adapt written materials to suit the reading ability of the children.

Labels and instruction cards. A common practice for introducing the written word into the classroom is to attach labels (on which are written single words, phrases or sentences) to various objects and work areas: door, window, the water trough, make a sandcastle, etc.

It is important that labels of this kind are changed periodically: familiar labels can be removed (and reintroduced later, if necessary) and new objects labelled; single word labels can be extended, where appropriate, to phrases and sentences; instructions can be altered, etc. The children should be alerted to these changes which should always reflect alterations in arrangements and activities in the classroom. Examples of labels and work cards which are changed when the activity or function of the work area changes include:

'open' or 'closed' sign on the shop;

'hospital', 'fire engine', 'kitchen' signs associated with the home corner;

'put a wall around the castle' assignment card relating to the sand tray;

'we found these on the beach'
'we found these in the park'   } captions relating to the nature table;

'put the animals in the red box'   } sorting tasks (colour names can be underlined
'put the clothes in the yellow box'   } with the appropriate colour)

Individual books. The compilation of the child's personal book can be an effective means of conveying to him the relevance and importance of the written word. A common procedure is for the teacher to write a caption (which is dictated by the child) under a painting, drawing or picture in his book. Topics are wide-ranging and might include a scene from a story, a place of interest recently visited, a collection of objects (either drawings of the objects or the objects themselves placed in a box), the family, and so on. Examples of captions:

the three pigs
the fire station
shells found on the beach
mum and dad
our dog

As children become familiar with the words and learn to recognize them, they can be encouraged to make use of a 'dictionary' of word cards from which they can select words to be written in their books.

Note. Suggestions relating to reading activities are contained in a number of pre-reading books. Useful guidance on the teaching of reading is contained in the Schools Council Linguistics and English Teaching; Initial Literacy Projects, *Breakthrough to literacy. Teacher's manual* by D. Mackay, B. Thompson and P. Schaub. Longman (1970).

Chapter 12   Stories, verses and songs

Introduction

Children's stories, verse and songs provide a wealth of material for encouraging language development. Associated activities such as music, mime, 'finger plays' and puppetry enhance the enjoyment and value of story and verse, and can be helpful in encouraging withdrawn and reticent children to participate. It is not possible within the limits of this short chapter to discuss stories and verses in detail. However, the following points should provide an introduction to the selection and use of suitable material.

Child's background. There is a very wide range of stories and verses from which to choose. Topics of fact and fantasy, human and animal characters, and settings such as city, suburb, country (farm) and seaside are generally well catered for in children's books. When choosing books it is important to bear in mind that some children have experience of only one type of setting; the child from the inner city might not be familiar with the suburb, country or seaside, while the country child might be equally unfamiliar with the city. Careful explanation and illustration will be necessary when reading stories, particularly if the setting is unfamiliar. Where possible, visits to new surroundings can be undertaken. Although pictures and illustrations are generally very helpful, there is a need for selection and explanation as some illustrations and caricatures tend to be too elaborate and overcrowded, and essential details are obscured.

Sequences. In the initial stages of story-telling the short sequences and pictures discussed on pages 29 and 30 can form a basis for longer narratives. In addition stories can be simplified by reducing them to the minimal amount of information: the main characters and events supported by about six key pictures. Here is an example of a traditional story, shortened and simplified.

The Gingerbread Man. (This story can be told in conjunction with sequence pictures such as those shown in the illustrations below. Each picture can be presented at the points indicated in the script.) An old woman and an old man lived in a little house. One day the old woman said 'I'm going to make a Gingerbread Man'. She took some dough and made a head, a body, two arms and two legs. (picture 1) She put the Gingerbread Man in the oven to bake. When the Gingerbread Man was baked the old lady opened the door. The Gingerbread Man jumped out of the oven and ran out of the house (picture 2) shouting 'Run, run, as fast as you can, you can't catch me I'm the Gingerbread Man.' The old woman and the old man ran after the Gingerbread Man but they could not catch him.

Soon the Gingerbread Man passed a cow. He said to the cow, 'Run, run as fast as you can, you can't catch me, I'm the Gingerbread Man.' The cow ran after the Gingerbread Man (picture 3), but it could not catch him. Next the Gingerbread Man passed a horse. He said to the horse, 'Run, run as fast as you can, you can't catch me, I'm the Gingerbread Man.' The horse ran after the Gingerbread Man (picture 4), but it could not catch him.

Then the Gingerbread Man saw a fox. He said to the fox, 'I've run away from an old woman, an old man, a cow and a horse, now I can run away from you'. But the fox said, 'Don't run away from me, you can jump on my back and I'll take you across the river'. So the Gingerbread Man jumped on the fox's back. The fox jumped into the river (picture 5) and started to swim to the other side. After they had gone a little way the fox said to the Gingerbread Man, 'You'll get wet on my back, you had better jump onto my nose so you can keep dry'. So the Gingerbread Man jumped onto the fox's nose (picture 6). Suddenly the fox threw the Gingerbread Man into the air, opened his mouth and snap, he ate up the Gingerbread Man (picture 7). The clever old fox was the only one who could catch the Gingerbread Man.

Shortened and simplified stories can be repeated at a later stage incorporating more details and more elaborate language. The child should also have the opportunity of listening to familiar stories (or new stories embracing vocabulary which is familiar to the child) without the support of illustrations so that the child will rely on the language to evoke the relevant imagery.

Language skills and traditional stories/verses

It is useful to look at traditional stories and verses in relation to some of the language skills (discussed in part 1) they can help develop. Many traditional stories and verses are characterized by certain patterns of rhythm and repetition which can help the child acquire important vocabulary and language patterns.

Naming, describing and categorising. The House that Jack Built, The Cat and the Mouse, Red Riding Hood, The Crooked Man and The Gingerbread Man are examples of stories and verses which can be used to focus on names (including items of food, parts of the body and face, animals, etc.), actions (including miming, swimming, building, milking etc.) and various colours, shapes and sizes.

Denoting position. Songs and rhymes accompanied by appropriate movements (dance, mime, puppets, and finger plays, etc.) can be used to focus on words and phrases such as up and down, round and round, in and out, over and under, backwards and forwards, nearer, further.

Sequencing. A clear sequence is central to many traditional stories and verses. Key events are often 'marked' or emphasized by the recurrence of certain language patterns. This repetition can help the child to follow the sequence by relating each event to preceding events, and to anticipate future events. The Three Pigs, The Three Kittens, The Gingerbread Man and The Cat and the Mouse are examples of narratives which can be used to focus on relational words of time (before, after, while, next etc.) and appropriate tenses.

PART 4

Checklist of language skills and Appendices

Checklist of language skills

Introduction
The purpose of the checklist is to help the teacher build up a picture of the child's language, based on observations during normal classroom activities. The checklist is not a standardised test, but a set of ratings which can provide a useful record of assessments of the child's language. On the checklist, language is broken down into a number of identifiable skills. These skills correspond to those discussed in part 1 so that the teacher can refer from the checklist to the appropriate parts of part 1.

The ratings on the checklist which describe the child's language skills are as follows:

Rating number	Description
1	good to very good
2	adequate
3	below average
4	poor or well below average

The ratings are intended to cover the language skills of children in general. It is therefore obvious that in some schools there will be a higher proportion of below average and well below average children than in other schools.

The first assessment of the child's language should be made as soon as possible after the initial settling-in period.

The ratings can be entered on the individual scoring sheet (see p. 82). Subsequent ratings, say towards the end of each term, would help to maintain a check on the child's progress. The checklist rates the seven language skills with which this handbook is concerned. Some of the skills are subdivided on the scoring sheet in order to enable a more careful rating of the child's development to be made, if required.

In addition, a space is provided for ratings of two other language characteristics, clarity of speech and comprehension.

Checklist of language skills (child's spoken language)
This part of the checklist concentrates on the child's productive (spoken) language, as distinct from his comprehension of language. Many of the language skills listed can be assessed by listening to the child's general conversation, and by asking questions about on-going activities.

Language skill 1: listening
1. Enjoys listening to stories: easy to hold a conversation.
2. Will listen with some interest. Can pay attention when required.
3. Often leaves an activity after a few seconds: cannot concentrate for long on a task; difficult to hold a reasonable conversation.
4. Restless and easily distracted: pays no attention to tasks required.

Language skill 2: naming (objects and actions)
1. Uses a wide variety of basic words.
2. Has a good grasp of vocabulary relating to common classroom materials (resources

and toys in work corners) and activities (walking, dressing, building, pouring, digging).
3. Has limited vocabulary.
4. Has a very limited vocabulary, and confuses the names of common objects and actions.

Language skill 3: categorising
1. Uses a variety of category words including, for example: furniture, vegetables, tools, musical instruments.
2. Uses commoner category words such as: people, animals, clothes, food.
3. Uses few category words.
4. Seldom/never uses category words; has little understanding of them.

Language skill 4: describing (colours)
1. Knows the names of a wide variety of colours and shades of colour (light/dark).
2. Knows common colour names such as: red, blue, yellow, green, brown, black, white.
3. Knows only a few colour names, but uses them correctly.
4. Confuses/does not know colour names.

Language skill 4: describing (shapes)
1. Can name a variety of shapes, including, for example, rectangular, triangular, curved, pointed.
2. Can name basic shapes such as: round, square, flat, straight, crooked.
3. Can name only a few shapes.
4. Cannot name shapes—appears confused by them.

Language skill 4: describing (size)
1. Uses a variety of words which denote size, such as: big, small, long, short, thin, thick, wide (and/or comparatives such as bigger than, longer than, thinner than).
2. Uses several words which denote size, such as: big, small, long, short (and/or comparatives such as bigger than, smaller than).
3. Seldom uses words which denote size, but is correct when they are used.
4. Seldom/never uses words which denote size; has little understanding of them.

Language skill 5: denoting position
1. Uses a wide variety of position words, including less common words such as: between, above, edge, opposite.
2. Uses commoner position words such as: on, in, next to, under, top, corner, side, middle.
3. Uses few position words.
4. Confuses position words—cannot follow them when used in instructions.

Language skill 6: sequencing
1. Can narrate lengthy sequences, without confusion.
2. Can narrate shorter sequences, without confusion.
3. Can narrate shorter sequences, but with some confusion.
4. Seldom/never attempts to sequence events; cannot follow sequence in instructions.

Language skill 6: linking sequence
1. Uses a wide variety of 'relational words of time' including less common words such as: while, as, until.
2. Uses commoner relational words of time such as: then, before, after, when, first.
3. Uses few relational words of time, mainly relying on then (and then).

4. Seldom/never uses relational words of time—is confused by them when used in instructions.

Language skill 6: using tenses
1. Uses a variety of tenses—various forms of present, past and future—including, for example: was running, will be able, is going to make, has taken, would like, might find.
2. Uses several tenses, but with less variety.
3. Uses one tense predominantly.
4. Tends to omit verbs; uses combinations such as: 'he big' (he's big), 'dog there' (dog was there), 'he home' (he has gone home).

Language skill 7: reasoning
1. Uses a variety of connectives including less common words such as: but, unless, though (even though).
2. Uses commoner connectives such as: if, because, so that, or.
3. Uses few connectives, mainly relying on: and, so.
4. Uses disconnected phrases and/or words.

Language skill 7: planning
1. Can give a detailed verbal plan of intentions—an account of all the stages, from the beginning to the final outcome, of an activity.
2. Can give a verbal plan of several stages of an activity.
3. Is confused about the next few stages of an activity.
4. Cannot describe the next step of an activity; little evidence of planning.

Clarity of speech

It is important that the child's pronunciation should not influence the teacher's assessment of his language skills on the checklist. It is possible that a child with pronunciation difficulties or differences nevertheless has a good vocabulary and uses elaborate language patterns. Many infant school children mispronounce words: e.g. 'wun' (run), 'thore' (sore), 'fings' (things), etc. Generally these are not regarded as serious defects, but as characteristics of immature speech. Moreover, regional accents are different from 'standard' pronunciation and these differences do not necessarily indicate any lack of skill in language usage. It is when the child's pronunciation seriously impairs verbal communication and discourages him from speaking, that special help is needed.

Pronunciation

1. Speech is very clear.
2. Speech is quite clear; some mispronunciations such as 'wun', 'thore', 'fings'.
3. Speech is difficult to understand.
4. Speech is incomprehensible.

Comprehension

It is of value, particularly in the case of the reticent child, to assess the child's understanding of language. This can usually be done by observing his ability to carry out instructions, and by observing his attentiveness during storytelling.

Comprehension of instructions (e.g. 'Go to the small cupboard and bring me the box on the top shelf.').
1. Carries out lengthy instructions in sequence and without omissions.
2. Carries out shorter instructions involving several objects and actions (as in the example above).
3. Confuses shorter instructions—needs prompting.
4. Cannot carry out simple instructions.

Attentiveness during story-telling
1. Is very attentive—even during long stories.
2. Is generally attentive during stories.
3. Is inattentive—easily distracted.
4. Is very inattentive—often bored or restless, and shows little interest in stories.

Additional assessment of language skills 5 and 6

The following materials and examples of questions can be used to assess the child's understanding of 'position' words (denoting position) and relational words of time (linking sequences) on the checklist.

Familiar objects such as a box, car, block, pencil and a sheet of paper can be used for questions relating to position and time.

Language skill 5: denoting position

Having named each object, the child is told that he is going to play a game of moving the toys. The teacher first demonstrates how the game is played by giving the instructions and carrying them out—putting the block in the box, the car next to the pencil, the pencil under the paper.

The child is then asked to carry out instructions such as:
Put the car on the paper.
Put the pencil behind the box.
Hold the block above the car.
Put the pencil between the car and the box.
With your finger touch a corner of the paper.
Touch an edge of the paper.
and so on, varying the materials and the 'position' words.

Language skill 6: linking sequences

The game is continued using the same materials, but the child is required to hand the toys to the teacher when asked.

Again the demonstration is one of giving the instructions and carrying them out— 'give me the car', 'first give me the block then give me the car'.

The child is then asked to carry out instructions such as:
First give me the box then give me the pencil.
Give me the car at the same time as the block.
Give me the pencil after you have given me the block.
Give me the box before you give me the pencil.
Give me the car while you are touching the box.
Before you give me the pencil, give me the box.
and so on, varying the materials and the linking 'time' words.

In order to assess the child's production of language the above games can be adapted so that the child is encouraged to follow the various movements and sequences and give a verbal commentary. Here are some examples of comments which could be encouraged:

'You put the car on the paper.'

'First you put the block in the box, then you put it under the box.'

'You opened the box before.'

Note. Several demonstrations and prompts might be necessary in order to convey the principle of the game.

It is suggested that teachers should produce sufficient copies of the checklist appearing on the opposite page to record the progress of each child in the class.

Individual scoring sheet for checklist

Name   Date of assessment
Date of birth   First
Date of school entry   Second
                                       Third
                                       Fourth

SKILLS	RATING SCALE			
	Good to very good	Adequate	Below average	Poor or well-below average
1. Listening				
2. Naming				
3. Categorising				
4. Describing colour				
shape				
size				
5. Denoting position				
6. Sequencing sequencing				
linking sequences				
using tenses				
7. Reasoning reasoning				
planning				
OPTIONAL				
Clarity of speech				
Comprehension—instructions				
Attentiveness—stories				

Place a cross in the appropriate square and join the crosses to form a profile. Several assessments can be plotted on the same scoring sheet, and a different colour can be used for each profile. The date of assessment and colour used to draw profile should be noted. If more than three or four profiles are drawn another scoring sheet will be needed.

APPENDICES

Appendix 1

Teachers' groups: their establishment and composition

During the winter term of 1969 the Programme Development Unit of the Project established four teachers' groups in local education authorities in England and Wales. Each group consisted of about eight to twelve members—mainly head teachers and class teachers. In addition the groups received regular and valuable support from LEA organisers and remedial advisers. The groups met regularly—about every five weeks—until the end of the summer term, 1971.

Aims

One of the first questions to be decided related to the type of material the groups should aim at producing. It was agreed, for the reasons set out in the preface, that it would be most fruitful to work towards the production of a handbook on language development plus some examples of ancillary materials such as language games. The handbook would contain aims, guidelines and suggestions rather than a programme containing numerous and detailed 'prescribed' activities and materials.

Discussions

Members of the groups were invited to bring to the meetings examples of descriptions of materials and activities used in their schools. These were discussed and ideas were exchanged. Specific activities were tried out in schools and the teachers reported on their findings. A member of the Project team visited schools regularly to observe and participate in these trials. Some teachers concentrated on one type of activity such as a work area ('corner') or a language game. At certain points in the discussions reference was made to language programmes such as Blank and Solomon, Bereiter and Engelmann. Although some features of the latter programme (particularly the repetition and drilling involved) were rejected for obvious reasons, it was generally agreed that some of the specific aims expressed in these programmes helped to clarify and sharpen the teachers' thinking about language.

Notes summarising the main discussion points were circulated to the groups. After several terms the papers were collated so that the many and wide-ranging aspects of language development and infant school activities which had been covered could be condensed and classified under a relatively small number of headings. The collated papers were then circulated and each language skill was discussed separately and further amendments were made. The collation procedure and the emergence of the language skills is summarised below.

Language skills

In order to achieve some kind of framework a number of broad categories of language were considered. One useful dichotomy is that of language reception and language production. With regard to vocabulary linguists such as Glanzer* refer to 'content' words (nouns, verbs, adjectives, adverbs) and 'function' words (pronouns, conjunctions, prepositions). The Blank and Solomon programme distinguishes between 'concrete' and 'abstract' functions of language. Another aspect of vocabulary highlighted in many programmes is the relational word—e.g. 'in', 'before' and 'if'—expressing relationships of space, time and cause-and-effect.

*Glanzer, M. (1962). 'Grammatical category: a role learning word
association analysis'. *Journal of verbal learning and verbal behaviour.* Vol. 1, 31–41.

The next stage in the collation procedure was to group the various activities and aspects of language which had been discussed in the meetings, using the above categories as a basis, and then to suggest more meaningful headings where appropriate.

Briefly the headings or skills which emerged and the areas of language covered are summarized as follows.

1 *Listening*. This refers to the wide range of activities designed to encourage the child to listen attentively and purposefully to various sounds—language and non-language sounds. An important aim is to improve the child's motivation and to encourage the reception of language (cf. skills 2 to 7 deal mainly with the production of language).

2 and 4 *Naming and Describing*. These skills refer to basic concrete vocabulary, i.e. the use of tangible everyday nouns, verbs and adjectives (these are referred to as 'content' words above.)

3 *Categorising*. This refers to the more abstract words used in classification, and which are relevant to certain sorting or grouping activities.
Examples of class concepts include animals, people, clothes.

5 *Denoting position*. This refers to the vocabulary of spatial relations, i.e. an object's position in relation to its surroundings. This involves the use of function and relational words referred to above.

6 *Sequencing*. This refers to vocabulary relating one event to another, and to the tenses involved. Activities include narrating stories and news. Function and relational words are central to this skill.

7 *Reasoning*. This refers to several interrelated aspects of language including words used in cause-and-effect relations, and the use of language of planning and hypothesising. This involves the use of function and relational words and the abstract use of language in the sense that it is separated from referents (see Blank and Solomon).

Language for thinking
It was felt that although skills 1, 2 and 4 are important and that disadvantaged children needed help in these areas of language, they are nevertheless relatively easier to acquire than skills 3, 5, 6 and 7. The latter skills are more abstract and more likely to be glossed over. Skills 3, 5, 6 and 7 cover the cognitive functions of language, that is language for thinking, for organising experience and planning activities.

Summary
It was agreed that although language is a unified whole it is useful to have a breakdown of this highly complex process into a number of easily recognisable skills which could be related to familiar activities in the infant school. This classification helped the teachers to be more aware of the nature of language and to think systematically about the purpose and relevance of activities and materials provided for children. Moreover the classification of language to a large extent counteracted the vagueness of terms such as 'fluency', 'creative language', 'free expression', 'elaboration' and 'vocabulary' which are often used rather loosely in discussions about language.

Appendix 2

Field trial of handbook and materials

During the spring term (January to April) 1971 thirty-two infant schools in four local education authorities in England and Wales took part in field testing an experimental version of the handbook and materials. At the end of the term each teacher completed a questionnaire (see p. 87) relating mainly to the usefulness of the handbook and materials in the classroom. The teachers were also asked to make specific comments and suggestions for improvements. Some of the suggestions proved most useful and were incorporated in the final draft of the handbook.

Although some of the schools involved in the field trial had also been involved in the discussion groups (mentioned in appendix 1), most of the teachers who tried out the experimental version of the handbook and materials had little or no involvement in the discussions and the handbook/materials were therefore new to them. It was hoped that these teachers would view the materials more objectively and critically than those involved in the discussion groups.

Because of the limited time available each teacher was asked to read through the handbook and examine the materials, and then to concentrate on one aspect of the handbook or materials in the classroom (see question 5 of the questionnaire, p. 87). The teachers worked with small groups of children or individuals in reception classes. The teachers were asked to select those children whom they regarded as 'disadvantaged' in terms of their home background, language development and general ability (see question 2 of the questionnaire). The age range of the children was from 4 years 7 months to 5 years 2 months.

Checklist of language skills

The checklist of language skills (see pages 78–80) was compiled and field tested separately, and at an earlier stage in the development of the handbook. This work was carried out by the teachers' groups. Three main stages were involved and are summarised as follows.

Stage 1. The teachers conducted a number of simple tests with the children which involved carrying out instructions and answering questions.

Stage 2. The questions and tests which had proved to be appropriate at stage 1 were grouped under headings which correspond to those used for the language skills. The areas of language covered by the questions were defined (examples of vocabulary were given) and a four-point rating scale was provided.

Stage 3. The checklist, in much the same form as it now appears in the handbook, was field tested in schools and a few amendments were made in the light of resulting comments.

Results of field testing

Note that this questionnaire format summarises the returns from the 32 schools. The totals in the item response categories do not always correspond to 32, since each school concentrated on one or two parts of the handbook, and no school covered all of it.

Note also that as a result of the responses to this questionnaire—especially the 'general comments'— modifications were made to the handbook and materials before this final version was produced.

**Schools Council Research and Development Project in Compensatory Education
Language development and the disadvantaged child.
A handbook for teachers of children in the first year of the infant school.**

Questionnaire

Name of school..32 schools ....
Name of class teacher/head teacher ....32 teachers...............................
    Please answer the following questions. Your comments will be helpful in compiling the
final version of the handbook/materials.

	Please tick
1. Number of children selected	
(a) 1 to 5	30
(b) 6 to 10	2
(c) 11 to 15	0
(d) over 15	0
2. On what basis were the children selected?	
(a) below average in intelligence	0
(b) below average in language development	3
(c) below average in quality of home background	1
(d) a combination of (a), (b) and (c)	28
(e) below average in age	0
(f) any other reason (please specify)	0
3. Length of time the handbook/materials were used each day:	
(a) up to 10 minutes	0
(b) up to 20 minutes	11
(c) up to 30 minutes	12
(d) up to 40 minutes	9
(e) more than 40 minutes (please specify)	0
4. Number of weeks during which the handbook/materials were in use:	
(a) up to 2 weeks	0
(b) up to 4 weeks	0
(c) up to 6 weeks	8
(d) up to 8 weeks	22
(e) more than 8 weeks (please specify)	2
5. On which part of the handbook/materials did you concentrate?	
(a) Part 1: language skills 1, 2, 4	8
(b) Part 1: language skills 3, 5, 6, 7	15
(c) Part 2: work areas	10
(d) materials/language games in Part 3	15
(e) Part 3: tape, reading, stories	5
6. Usefulness of handbook as a whole:	
(a) very useful	19
(b) generally useful	10
(c) fairly useful	3
(d) of little use	0
7. Clarity of handbook:	
(a) very clear, easy to follow	29
(b) generally clear	2
(c) fairly clear	1
(d) not clear, difficult to follow	0

8. Usefulness of materials/language games in Part 3 (answer if applicable):
   (a) very useful | 7
   (b) generally useful | 3
   (c) fairly useful | 2
   (d) of little use | 3

9. Usefulness of tape and accompanying notes (answer if applicable):
   (a) very useful | 2
   (b) generally useful | 3
   (c) fairly useful | 0
   (d) of little use | 0

Answer either 10 and 11 or 12 and 13

10. Children's response to activities in handbook (excluding materials/ language games in Part 3):
   (a) activities were very interesting and enjoyable | 20
   (b) activities were on the whole interesting and enjoyable | 10
   (c) activities were fairly interesting and enjoyable | 2
   (d) activities were not interesting and enjoyable | 0

11. Effectiveness of activities in handbook (excluding materials/language games in Part 3)
   (a) children made considerable progress in the language skills dealt with | 2
   (b) children made some progress in the language skills dealt with | 15
   (c) children made a little progress in the language skills dealt with | 0
   (d) children made no progress in the language skills dealt with | 0

12. Children's response to materials/language games in Part 3:
   (a) games were very interesting and enjoyable | 8
   (b) games were on the whole interesting and enjoyable | 4
   (c) games were fairly interesting and enjoyable | 3
   (d) games were not interesting and enjoyable | 0

*13. Effectiveness of materials/language games in Part 3:
   (a) children made considerable progress in the language skills dealt with | 1
   (b) children made some progress in the language skills dealt with | 11
   (c) children made a little progress in the language skills dealt with | 0
   (d) children made no progress in the language skills dealt with | 0

*Many of the teachers preferred not to rate the effectiveness of the handbook/materials because of the limited duration of the trial.

14. The routine use of handbook/materials:
   (a) best used for approximately 20 minute periods regularly each day | 10
   (b) best used occasionally: fitted into classroom routine when convenient | 4
   (c) best used for 20 minute periods regularly each day, and in addition fitted into classroom routine when convenient | 18
   (d) any other routine (please specify) | 0

Teachers were also asked to comment on any difficulties, ambiguities or omissions in the handbook and materials.

Bibliography

Bereiter, C. and Engelmann, S. (1966) *Teaching Disadvantaged Children in the Preschool* Englewood Cliffs, New Jersey: Prentice-Hall

Blank, M. and Solomon, F. (1968) "A tutorial language programme to develop abstract thinking in socially disadvantaged preschool children" in *Child Development* 39, pp. 379–389

Blank, M. and Solomon, F. (1969) "How shall the disadvantaged be taught?" in *Child Development* 40, pp. 47–61

Carroll, J. B. (1960) "Language development in children" in *Enclyclopaedia of Educational Research*, ed. Ebel New York: Collier-Macmillan

Carroll, J. B. (1964) *Language and Thought.* Englewood Cliffs, New Jersey: Prentice-Hall

Cazden, C. B. (1968) "Some implications of research and language development for pre-school education" in *Early Education: Current Theory, Research and Practice*, ed. Hess and Bear Chicago: Aldine

Gahagan, D. M. and Gahagan, G. A. (1970) *Talk Reform: Explorations in Language for Infant School Children* London: Routledge and Kegan Paul

Gray, S. W. et al (1966) *Before First Grade: Training Project for Culturally Disadvantaged Children* New York: Teachers College Press

Halliday, M. A. K. (1969) "Relevant models of language" in *The State of Language*, ed. Wilkinson University of Birmingham School of Education

Inhelder, B. and Piaget, J. (1964) *The Early Growth of Logic in the Child* London: Routledge and Kegan Paul

Jensen, A. R. (1968) "Social class and verbal learning" in *Social Class, Race and Psychological Development*, ed. Deutsch et al New York: Irvington

Labov, W. (1970) "The logic of non-standard English" (chapter 9) in *Language and Poverty: Perspectives of a Theme*, ed. Williams New York: Academic Press

Lewis, M. M. (1951) *Infant Speech* London: Routledge and Kegan Paul

Loban, W. D. (1963) *The Language of Elementary School Children*, Champaign, Ill, U.S.A. National Council of Teachers of English

Luria, A. R. (1961a) *The Role of Speech in the Regulation of Normal and Abnormal Behaviour* New York: Irvington

Luria, A. R. (1961b) "The genesis of voluntary movements" in *Recent Soviet Psychology*, ed. O'Connor New York: Liveright

McNeill, D. (1966) "The creation of language" in *Language*, ed. Oldfield and Marshall Harmondsworth: Penguin Books

Moss, M. N. (1973) ``Deprivation and disadvantage?'' Block 8 of *Language and Learning* Bletchley: Open University Press

Razran, G. (1961) ``The observable unconscious and the inferable conscious in current Soviet psychophysiology: interoceptive conditioning, semantic conditioning and the orienting reflex'' in *Psychological Review* 68, pp. 81–147

Templin, M. C. (1957) *Certain Language Skills in Children: Their Development and Inter-relationships* (University of Minnesota Institute of Child Welfare Monographs no. 26, reprint 1975 of 1957 edn.) Westport, Conn.: Greenwood

Tough, J. (1976a) *The Development of Meaning: A Study of Children's use of Language* London: Allen and Unwin

Tough, J. (1976b) *Listening to Children Talking: A Guide to the Appraisal of Children's Use of Language* London: Ward Lock Educational for the Schools Council

Tough, J. (1977) *Talking and Learning: A Guide to Fostering Communication Skills in Nursery and Infant Schools* London: Ward Lock Educational for the Schools Council

Vygotsky, I. S. (trans. Haufmann and Vakar) (1962) *Thought and Language* Cambridge, Mass.: M.I.T. Press

Wilkinson, A. (1971) *The Foundation of Language: Talking and Reading in Young Children* (pp. 39–44) Oxford University Press

Index of games

N: Naming   D: Describing   DP: Denoting position   R: Reasoning
L: Listening   C: Categorising   S: Sequencing
(Rd: these two games are included in the section on Reading, pp. 72–3)
Figures in bold denote illustration